It Takes Two to Talk

It Takes Two to Talk

*A Practical Guide
for Parents
of Children with
Language Delays*

Jan Pepper and Elaine Weitzman

based on the third edition by Ayala Hanen Manolson

The
Hanen
Program®

It Takes Two to Talk®
By Jan Pepper and Elaine Weitzman

The
Hanen
Program®

A Hanen Centre Publication

The Hanen Program®, The Parent-Child Logo and It Takes Two to Talk® are trademarks owned by Hanen Early Language Program.

© Hanen Early Language Program, 2004.
Fourth Edition

Library and Archives Canada Cataloguing in Publication

ISBN 0-921145-19-5

Copies of this book may be ordered from the publisher:

THE HANEN CENTRE
1075 Bay Street, Suite 515
Toronto, Ontario
Canada M5S 2B1
Telephone: (416) 921-1073
Fax: (416) 921-1225
E-mail: info@hanen.org
Web: www.hanen.org

Parts of this book were adapted from two other Hanen Centre publications, *More Than Words* (Sussman, 1999) and *Learning Language and Loving It* (Weitzman & Greenberg, 2002). Information on "Create opportunities for your child to lead" (Ch 2), "Create opportunities for your child to take turns" (Ch 7), Cues (Ch 4), SPARK (Ch 5), The 4 Ss, and Visual Helpers was adapted from *More Than Words*. Information on Cues, including Questions (Ch 4, 5, 8, 9), Three Kinds of Play and Adding Ideas to Pretend Play (Ch 7), and much of the information in Chapter 8 on Sharing Books, including the "language of learning" and laying the foundations for reading and writing, was adapted from *Learning Language and Loving It*.

Illustrations: Pat Cupples
Design: Counterpunch / Linda Gustafson, Peter Ross
Editor: Martin Townsend

Printed in Canada by: Transcontinental Interglobe

To Hanen Certified speech-language

pathologists/therapists around the world,

who make such a difference in the lives

of children with language delays and

their families.

Contents

Foreword

Welcome to *It Takes Two to Talk*! If you have picked up this book, you are probably thinking hard about the speech and language development of an important young child in your life. You might also be worrying about this child, wondering why he or she might not be developing communication skills at the expected rate, and how you could help him or her move forward in this area of development. You have the right book in your hands!

It Takes Two to Talk is a book for parents and caregivers of young children who need extra support in their speech and language development. It is a book that will teach you skills and strategies that you can use on a daily basis, in almost every interaction you have with your child. The book has been written by speech-language pathologists who realize that parents can, in many ways, contribute to their child's speech and language development more than the professionals. We are the constant people in our young children's lives. We are there more than the professionals. What this book does is give us the strategies the professionals use so that our children can benefit from long-term, ongoing, daily support.

Take your time with reading the book. There is so much to learn, and many of the ideas and strategies take time to practice. But as you practice them, your child will benefit. Be open to interacting with your child in new ways, observing gestures and facial expressions carefully and following his or her lead. Like many things in life, the more you put into working with the *It Takes Two to Talk* Program, the more you will get out of it, and the more your child will benefit. It is not a hard program to learn. It just takes some time and practice.

Do not feel alone in your world of having a child with delayed speech and language. This book was written because there are many, many children who, for various reasons, have delayed speech and language. This book will help you and, in turn, will help your child. It will be exciting, and it will be wonderful. Celebrate all of the small steps, because together they add up to moving forward. Your child is fortunate because you have taken the time to pick up this book and learn from it. You want to support your child, and this book is here to help you do that. Enjoy your reading and, more important, enjoy communicating with your child!

Anne Marie
It Takes Two to Talk parent

Acknowledgements

Jan Pepper would like to say ...

Ayala Hanen Manolson, the first Executive Director of The Hanen Centre and author of this book's earlier editions, had the wisdom to see the importance of involving parents when she founded The Hanen Centre in 1977. Her creativity started a legacy that has helped thousands of children, families and speech-language professionals around the world.

I owe my greatest thanks to the families I have worked with over the years. This book is for parents, whose devotion is a constant source of inspiration, and for children who face the challenge of communicating when it doesn't come easily. It is for you that I wanted this book to be everything it could be.

My colleagues at The Hanen Centre make it a pleasure to come to work every day. I would especially like to thank Cindy Conklin, Cindy Earle, Janice Greenberg, Michelle Lintott, Cheri Rorabeck, Sandra Strachan and Fern Sussman for their ideas and support throughout this project. I would also like to thank Penny Tantakis and Stacie Scherer for their creative work in design and production. Behind the words in this book is a talented group of Hanen Instructors who bring *It Takes Two to Talk* to life all over the world by training and inspiring speech-language pathologists. Thank you for so generously sharing your ideas, reviewing chapter drafts and providing feedback. I am grateful to Barb Wylde and the speech-language pathologists with the south quadrant of Toronto Preschool Speech and Language Services and to Diana Ingrosso and Bonnie Stewart of Early Words in Hamilton, Ontario, for their time and suggestions.

I would like to thank Dr. Luigi Girolametto for his scholarly support in helping to make sure that this revision reflects the most current theory in child language disorders and early intervention.

There is much more to writing a book than putting words on paper. Martin Townsend is a gifted editor who took our words and made them sound better without changing what we wanted to say. Pat Cupples made the words come to life in her delightful illustrations, which serve as "visual helpers" throughout this book. I would also like to thank Linda Gustafson at Counterpunch for her thoughtfulness, patience and eye for detail in the design of this book.

I would like to thank my family for giving me such a wonderful example of how every child can thrive when surrounded by people who love and care for her. Mom shared her love of learning. Thank you for persuading me to "look it up in the dictionary." Dad encouraged me to make life an adventure and never stop seeing the wonder of the world.

It is difficult to find words to adequately express thanks to my friends for their constant support, love and encouragement over the years. Their children – a whole new generation of friends – have provided a source of joy and laughter in my life and have given me the opportunity to see the world through the eyes of a child. In many different ways, they are an important part of this book.

Finally, a heartfelt thank you to Maddie, Lee-Ann and James for their important contribution to *It Takes Two to Talk*.

Elaine Weitzman would like to say ...

I would like to thank the Hanen team, who always go above and beyond the call of duty when such a major project has to get done. Thanks to Vilia Cox, Tom Khan, Kamila Lear, Teresa Sartori, Sara Coutinho, Stacie Scherer, Janice Greenberg, Michelle Lintott, Laurie Kientz, Ryan McKnight, Anita DaSilva and Barb Wylde. Each of you contributed in some important way to getting this guidebook done. I would especially like to thank Penny Tantakis, Marketing Manager, for taking on the task of production of this guidebook and for being willing to drop everything whenever necessary to keep production on schedule.

Special thanks go to three good friends, who are also talented clinicians and wonderful colleagues. Fern Sussman and Cindy Earle provided invaluable input into Chapter 7 at a time when they were both immersed in other projects. Anne McDade, Hanen UK/Ireland Representative and Hanen Instructor, came up with the SPARK acronym all the way from Scotland (thank goodness for instant messaging and e-mail) and was always available to provide input at a moment's notice, in spite of the time difference.

The Hanen Centre is fortunate to have the support and guidance of a committed Board of Directors. Many thanks to Jim Wooder, Chairman, Edmund Clarke, Frank Copping, Liz Milne, Juli Morrow and Derek Nelson for their ongoing interest in and commitment to our growing organization.

Thanks go to my wonderful family. My mother, who was the model of a career woman long before her time, has always encouraged me and continues to take an active interest in whatever I do. My sisters, Adele and Margie, are a source of ongoing support and always provide welcome comic relief.

My daughter, Joanne, kept me going with our nightly on-line chats while we both worked at our computers in different cities. She has taught me a great deal about communication and perseverance, and her interest and encouragement sustained me in more ways than she realizes. My son, Kevin, who is living it up in Montreal and whom I miss so much, always brightened up my days with his intermittent calls and visits. Writing Chapter 8 brought back wonderful memories of when he was little and when he used to demand that I read his favourite books to him again and again. And finally, to my husband, Irvine, my anchor and my sanity, who doesn't really like being thanked, all I can say is I couldn't do it without you.

Chapter 1

Learn More About Your Child's Communication

These children all have something important to say, but they can't express themselves as well or as easily as other children their age. Perhaps you have something in common with the parents of these children. Like them, you want what's best for your child. You want to help your child communicate. If you are the parent or caregiver of a child whose speech and language are not developing as expected, *It Takes Two to Talk* is for you.

You've Already Started

Children don't learn to talk all by themselves. They learn to communicate gradually as they spend time with the important people in their lives, especially their parents. You and your child have been communicating since he was born. Through this communication you've developed a strong connection. To help him become the best communicator he can be, you just need to build on the connection you already have.

By reading *It Takes Two to Talk,* you'll learn simple but powerful strategies for helping your child communicate to the best of his ability. You'll find that everyday situations like getting him dressed or putting him to bed are ideal times to use these strategies. What's more, you'll see that building communication into your child's everyday life won't be hard work or stressful – for your child or for you. In fact, it will become a natural part of the time you spend together.

How and Why Children Communicate

Communication isn't just about talking. Whenever two people send messages of any kind to each other – even without words – they are communicating. Babies communicate long before they start to talk – by crying, making sounds, moving their bodies or reaching for something. As children grow, they let you know what's on their minds in other ways, such as through gestures, speech and signs. Learning more about **how** your child communicates is the first step toward helping him become a better communicator.

HOW Colin communicates with his mom: by looking at her, smiling and wiggling his arms and legs.

Uh.

HOW Brian communicates with his dad: he looks, points and makes a sound.

Becoming aware of **how** your child communicates is important, but you also need to think about **why** he communicates. Even before they use words, children communicate for many different reasons: to tell you what they want or don't want, to get your attention, to ask questions or to make comments. As their communication develops, they get better at letting you know what's on their minds and what's important to them.

WHY Alicia communicates: to ask her mom a question.

WHY Graham communicates: to make a comment about his tractor.

WHY Adam communicates: to tell his dad he doesn't want something.

Signs and pictures

When children understand what words mean but are having a hard time learning to talk, they can learn to communicate by making signs or pointing to pictures instead. Throughout this book, you'll read more about how signs and pictures can help children learn language. A speech-language professional can help you decide whether this approach could benefit your child.

Learning more about how and why your child communicates will help you see and hear the messages he sends you — even the ones that aren't so obvious. The following lists describe **how** and **why** children communicate. Circle or highlight the hows and whys you notice in your child.

HOW My Child Communicates:

★ Cries or screams ★ Smiles ★ Moves his body (kicks, wiggles) ★ Changes his facial expression ★ Makes sounds ★ Reaches ★ Looks at me or at what he wants ★ Points ★ Imitates sounds ★ Looks at what he wants and then at me ★ Takes me by the hand to what he wants ★ Uses gestures, such as waving for bye-bye ★ Uses sounds that stand for words ★ Uses single words or signs ★ Combines two or more words at a time

WHY My Child Communicates:

★ Because he is hungry or tired ★ Because he is happy ★ To respond to something interesting, such as my voice ★ To protest or refuse something ★ To get attention ★ To request something ★ To show me something he is interested in ★ To greet or say goodbye ★ To show off ★ To follow directions ★ To answer questions ★ To tell someone about something (comment) ★ To ask a question

Your Child's Stage of Communication

Every child's ability to communicate develops gradually over time. In *It Takes Two to Talk,* we divide the early years of this development into four major stages:

- **Discoverers** react to how they feel and to what is happening around them, but do not communicate with a specific purpose in mind.
- **Communicators** send specific messages without using words.
- **First Words Users** use single words (or signs or pictures).
- **Combiners** combine words into sentences of two or three words.

Children with communication difficulties progress through the same stages as other children, but more slowly (although some children may not get through all the stages).

As you read the descriptions of the four stages below, think about which one best describes how and why your child is currently communicating.

Discoverer

How the Discoverer Expresses Himself:
The Discoverer is in the earliest stage of learning to communicate. He does not yet communicate deliberately (with a specific purpose in mind). He just reacts to how he is feeling and to what is happening around him. In the beginning, crying is the best way a Discoverer has to let you know that he needs something, such as food, sleep or to be picked up. Over time his cries change, and a "hungry cry" sounds different from a "tired cry."

From watching the way Jordan looks at his smiley-face pillow, his mom can tell that he really likes it.

The Discoverer also communicates through facial expressions and body movements. He may turn away if he doesn't want something. If there's too much going on, he may close his eyes. Soon, the Discoverer learns to stop moving so that he can pay attention to new and interesting sights, sensations and sounds, including the sound of your voice. He becomes interested in others and expresses this interest by looking, smiling or making sounds. Later on, the Discoverer begins to explore his world more. He reaches for objects or people, or moves toward them. Parents have to pay close attention to learn what a Discoverer is interested in.

The Discoverer begins to use his voice in different ways. The first sounds that he makes are sounds like "eeee" and "aaah." Later, these change to sounds like "coo" and "goo." This is called cooing. Toward the end of the stage, the Discoverer puts together strings of sounds like "bah-bah-bah-bah-bah." This is called babbling.

The Discoverer also changes the loudness and tone of his voice. He may make happy sounds when you talk or sing to him. He also imitates some of the sounds you make, as well as some of your actions and facial expressions. The Discoverer looks, smiles, laughs and makes sounds to get and keep your attention. You can tell that he enjoys interacting with you.

What the Discoverer Understands: The Discoverer doesn't yet understand words, but he's becoming more aware of the world around him. He is starting to recognize some faces, objects, voices and sounds. He turns his head toward some sounds and voices, especially Mom's or Dad's. He is easily startled by sudden changes, such as loud noises or fast movements.

The Discoverer smiles back at a face that is smiling at him. He watches your face when you talk to him. An older Discoverer stops moving when he hears you call his name and also starts to understand simple gestures. For example, when you hold your arms out, he may lift his arms to be picked up. Although the Discoverer doesn't yet understand your words, he responds to the tone of your voice and to familiar situations. Over time, he begins to anticipate what happens next in daily routines like meals or bath time. For example, when you're getting him ready for his bath and he hears the water running, he may squeal or kick his legs because he's looking forward to splashing in the tub. Because he can anticipate, the Discoverer also enjoys games like Peekaboo and Tickle.

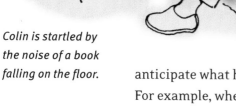

Colin is startled by the noise of a book falling on the floor.

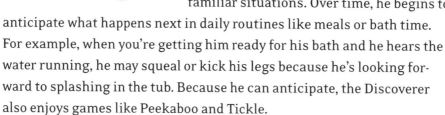

Communicator

When you consistently respond to your child's messages, gradually he makes the exciting and powerful connection that what he does has an effect on those around him. He now understands that he can make things happen. For example, he realizes that when he holds his arms up, you pick him up, and when he makes a sound, you pay attention to him. Reaching this new understanding of the world is called making the **communication connection.** When your child makes the communication connection, he becomes a Communicator.

How the Communicator Expresses Himself: The Communicator begins to send messages with a specific purpose in mind. Even though he isn't using words yet, he communicates with you by looking at you, making gestures, pointing and making sounds. At first, he communicates to protest or refuse something he doesn't want. He'll also let you know that he wants an object – a toy, for instance – or that he wants you to do something, like take him out of his high chair.

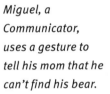

Later on, the Communicator becomes more social in his communication, sharing his interests with you. He communicates to get your attention, to say hello or goodbye, or to show you something. Often he'll point to tell you about something. He may also make sounds in a questioning tone of voice to ask questions. As he gets better and better at communicating with you, he may even make up his own gestures. For example, if he rubs his face with the back of his hand, he may be communicating about his special blanket.

Miguel, a Communicator, uses a gesture to tell his mom that he can't find his bear.

The Communicator may keep trying to get his message across until you respond the way he wants. For example, if he reaches and makes sounds to ask for a cracker and you hand him a cracker, he may become quiet. He may also smile to let you know that's what he wants. But if he wants a cracker and you hand him a drink, he'll often let you know that's not what he wants. He might appear quite frustrated, raising his voice. He may take your hand to show you exactly what he wants. Succeeding at making himself understood is an important part of his communication development.

Another important part of his development happens when he learns to focus on a person and an object at the same time. Previously, your child could focus on either you or an object, but not both together. At the Communicator stage he looks at an object and points to it, and then he looks at you. Then he looks back and points to the object again, to make sure you know what he's communicating about. This new skill makes it possible for him to show you things and let you know what he thinks about them. This is one of the most important steps on the way to using first words or signs.

Robert lets his grandmother know what's on his mind by pointing to the apple while looking first at her and then back at the apple.

The Communicator also learns to follow *your* focus. If you point to something, he can look in that direction to see what you're showing him. Now you can point out lots of interesting things – creating all kinds of opportunities for language learning.

The Communicator continues to make sounds, imitating your sounds more often. He starts to put sounds together and almost seems to be talking. But his "talking" is all sounds and no words. He may also make sounds that are his first deliberate attempts to use words.

By looking up, Adam lets his mom know that he understands the word light.

What the Communicator Understands: As the Communicator experiences everyday activities, like getting dressed or going to bed, he hears you say certain words over and over again. In time he'll begin to understand what they mean. He'll let you know he understands by looking, pointing, showing or following your simple directions. This is an important part of language development because your child needs to understand a word before he can use it to communicate.

First Words User

How the First Words User Expresses Himself: It's exciting when your child uses his first word. This is a moment parents wait for, especially if language has been slow to develop. The First Words User may imitate words that he hears you say, or he may begin to use words all by himself. He starts by saying one word at a time. (Children who communicate by making one sign at a time or by pointing to one picture at a time are also First Words Users.) These first words represent people, objects and actions that are familiar and important in your child's world, like *mama, dada, juice, doggie* or *up*. Along with these words he'll continue to use gestures, sounds and facial expressions. A First Words User may also use one word for many different things. *Juice* might refer to any drink. *Doggie* might refer to any animal with four legs and a tail.

The First Words User uses one word to express a whole message. If he points to a chair and says "Mama," he might mean either "That's Mommy's chair" or "Sit here, Mommy." You can figure out what he means by looking at the whole situation and tuning in to his actions, tone of voice, gestures and facial expressions.

Your child's first words may be simpler versions of real words, like *nana* for *banana* or *teep* for *sleep*. You'll learn what they mean because whenever he sees or experiences these things, he'll say the words the same way. It may be difficult to figure out what some of your child's early words mean. Once you figure them out, you may be the only person who recognizes them.

Ball *is Scott's word for anything that is round.*

Elizabeth's Mom figured out that "dee-dee" means kitty *after hearing Elizabeth say it a few times whenever she saw a cat.*

What the First Words User Understands: The First Words User's understanding of words continues to grow during this stage. He can point to or show you familiar objects and people when you say their names. He also understands simple directions and phrases like "Get your cup" or "Time for your bath," especially if you use gestures with your words.

Combiner

How the Combiner Expresses Himself: Often (but not always) by the time a child uses about 50 single words, signs or pictures, he's ready to begin putting them together in combinations like "More juice" or "Mommy up." These two-word combinations sometimes send a clear message, as in "Want teddy." However, as these three illustrations show, you may need to look for clues to figure out exactly what a Combiner means.

Here, *"Daddy shoe" means "Those are Daddy's shoes."*

Here, *"Daddy shoe" means "Daddy, put my shoes on."*

Here, *"Daddy shoe" means "I'm wearing Daddy's shoes."*

At first the Combiner continues to use single words along with two-word combinations. He relies less and less on gestures to get his message across. He learns to change his word combinations into questions by changing the tone of his voice. For instance, "Cookie allgone?" might mean "Are the cookies all gone?" He also begins to ask questions like "What that?" or "Where kitty?"

What the Combiner Understands: The Combiner understands many simple instructions without the help of gestures. He can also identify an object not only by its name, but by what you do with it. For example, he can point to food when you ask, "Show me what you eat." He understands simple questions that start with *where, what* and *who*. He is also beginning to understand words like *in, on, under, big* and *little*. He listens to short, simple stories and can point to familiar objects pictured in books.

Learning to communicate is a journey and it takes time. To see where your child is on this journey now, fill out the following checklist.

My Child's Stage of Communication Development

To learn more about your child's communication, complete the following checklist. As you read the statements, put an *A, O, R* or *N* next to each one to show how well it describes your child.

A = Always
O = Often
R = Rarely
N = Never

Sometimes a child's ability to **understand** language is more developed than his ability to **express** himself. So it's possible that your child may be at one stage for expression and a more advanced stage for understanding.

Discoverer	*Understanding**	*Expression*
	MY CHILD … __ looks at me when I talk or sing softly to him. __ smiles when I smile at him or talk to him. __ recognizes familiar voices. __ turns his head toward sounds he hears. __ responds when I call his name by looking at me, moving his body or holding still. __ recognizes a few gestures (such as gestures for *up* or *no*). __ anticipates the next step in daily routines.	MY CHILD … __ cries or fusses when he is sleepy, hungry or uncomfortable. __ has different cries, depending on what he needs. __ makes sounds when he is spoken to or smiled at. __ makes vowel sounds like "ah," "uh" and "eh." __ makes consonant sounds like "buh," "guh" or "ma." __ imitates some sounds he hears. __ imitates me back when I imitate a sound that he makes. __ imitates simple actions, for instance banging on the tray of his high chair. __ babbles, repeating sounds like "ba-ba-ba" or "nuh-nuh-nuh." __ closes his eyes or turns away when he doesn't want something. __ looks at, reaches for or moves toward objects or people he's interested in.
	* *Discoverers don't yet understand what words mean.*	

→ Say less
→ stress
→ Show
→ slow

Communicator	*Understanding*	*Expression*
	MY CHILD ... ☑ understands familiar words in routine situations, like *bye-bye* or *up*. ☑ understands names of familiar objects, like *bottle*, *light* or *cookie*. ☑ responds to simple questions like "Where's your teddy bear?" by moving to the object, looking at it or pointing to it. ☑ can follow simple directions accompanied by gestures (such as when you wave and say, "Wave bye-bye"). ☑ understands the meaning of *no*.	MY CHILD ... ☑ takes me by the hand and pulls me toward objects that he wants. ☑ draws my attention to objects and people by giving or showing them to me or pointing to them. ☑ imitates actions such as clapping. ☑ imitates sounds. ☑ uses a few gestures, such as shaking his head for no or waving goodbye. ☑ looks at or points to what he wants or is interested in, and then looks at me. ☑ makes sounds that resemble words. ☑ puts strings of sounds together that almost sound like speech (called "jargon").
First Words User	*Understanding*	*Expression*
	MY CHILD ... ☑ can point to familiar body parts and objects. ☑ follows simple instructions even without gestures (such as "Kiss the baby"). ☑ can answer yes-or-no questions, such as "Do you want a banana?" ☑ responds to questions like "Where's the cup?" ☑ understands the names of many familiar objects, people and animals.	MY CHILD ... ☑ uses at least three words (or signs, or points to pictures) to communicate. ☑ uses more gestures or sounds than he used to. ☑ imitates sounds (like those animals make) and words. ☑ uses between 10 and 25 words or signs. ☐ points to 10 or more pictures to send messages. ☐ uses 25 to 50 words or signs.

Combiner	Understanding	Expression
	MY CHILD ... __ can answer questions like "What do you wear on your feet?" __ understands questions that start with *who*, such as "Who is at the door?" __ understands the meaning of the following concepts: __ *in*, __ *on*, __ *under*, __ *big*, __ *little*. __ can sort objects by category, such as animals and toys. __ listens to simple stories.	MY CHILD ... __ combines two words or signs together, as in "Want juice" or "No bed." __ uses at least 50 words. __ asks questions using a rising tone (as in "Mommy sleepy?"). __ asks questions that start with *what* and *where*, like "What's that?" __ combines three words together, as in "Want more juice" or "Me no hat." __ refers to himself by his name.

Discoverer, Communicator, First Words User or Combiner?

Look for the highest stage under "Understanding" where you wrote down an *A* or an *O* for *at least three statements*. This is your child's stage of communication development for **understanding**.

Now look for the highest stage under "Expression" in which you marked an *A* or an *O* for the *first* statement in that list. This is your child's stage of communication development for **expression**.

As you read this book, you'll come across strategies that apply to a particular stage of communication development. **Usually, the stage to keep in mind will be your child's stage of expression.** In some later chapters, however, you'll be asked to select strategies according to your child's stage of understanding.

Chapter 2

Let Your Child Lead

When two people communicate back and forth, with or without words, they are taking part in an **interaction**. The best way to encourage your child to communicate is to let her *start* more interactions with you. Instead of leading or directing the interaction yourself, **let your child lead**.

When you let your child lead — and when you respond with interest to what she is telling you — she'll want to communicate with you even more. And that's not the only reason to let your child lead. Every time *she* leads an interaction and you respond to her, you give her information about things that interest her — information she needs to improve her communication. That's why we say, "Children who lead get the language they need."

Get Face to Face

The first step toward letting your child lead is to **get face to face**. When the two of you are face to face …

- you and your child can connect more easily and share the moment
- both of you can hear and see each other's messages better
- it's easier for you to encourage your child to take the lead

So whenever you can, make it easy for your child to look right into your eyes. Look at how these parents do it:

It's more fun face to face.

OWL to Let Your Child Lead

Letting your child lead begins with **OWL**:

Observe

Wait

Listen

The first letters of these three important words can help you remember them.

OWLing is an important strategy that you can use with your child throughout an interaction. When you OWL, you open up all sorts of opportunities for communication. You may even discover that your child is communicating more than you realized.

Observe, Wait and Listen: Taking the time to OWL is a wise way to start.

Observe

Sometimes it's hard to know what's on your child's mind. Taking the time to observe her body language – her actions, gestures and facial expressions – will help you figure it out. By tuning in to these messages, you can learn a lot about what she's interested in and what she wants to tell you. Notice what your child is looking at. Look in the direction in which she's reaching or pointing. Discovering what has captured your child's interest will help you share the moment with her.

Mom was trying to get Megan to look in the mirror, but then she observed that Megan was more interested in something else — her sock had come off. Now they can talk about what Megan is really interested in.

Wait

Waiting is a powerful tool. It gives you time to observe what your child is interested in. Even more importantly, it gives your child time to start an interaction or respond to what you've said or done. In this book, *wait* means three things: **stop talking, lean forward** and **look at your child expectantly.** Your child may be used to everyone else doing the communicating. Waiting in this way will send her the message that you're ready for her to respond to you or, better still, to take the lead herself. Once your child does one of these things, it's important for you to respond to her immediately. (You'll learn more about how to do this in Chapter 3.)

If you need to remind yourself to wait, count slowly to 10 — silently, of course. At first, you may not be used to that much silence. Your child may not be used to it either. But be patient and don't rush to say something. It may take some time for her to communicate with you. If your child switches from one activity to another, wait

Instead of answering the door when the doorbell rings, Robert's dad waits. This gives Robert a chance to tell him there's someone at the door.

again. Give her a chance to get involved in the new activity. Then give her still more time to start an interaction.

The most important thing to remember about waiting is to give your child enough time to understand that you expect her to send you a message — any message. It doesn't matter whether she sends it with sounds, words or gestures. Anything that your child does or says to make her needs or interests known to you is a message. Take another look at the Expression side of the checklist you completed in Chapter 1, "My Child's Stage of Communication Development." There you'll find some of the ways in which your child may send a message.

Listen

Listening means paying close attention to all of your child's words and sounds. Take care not to interrupt her, even if you've already figured out what she's telling you. When you listen to your child's message, you're also letting her know that what she says is important to you. This helps build her confidence and self-esteem.

Even when you OWL, there will be times when you cannot understand your child's message. This can be frustrating for both of you. At times like these, look at the situation for clues and guess what she's trying to tell you.

Elizabeth's mom listens carefully and realizes that Elizabeth is trying to say Kitty.

If you can't even begin to guess your child's message, imitate her sounds or actions and then wait to see if she does anything to make her message clearer. You may still not understand, but it's important to make the effort. When you do, you let her know that you're trying your best to understand her. You're also showing her that what's on her mind is very important to you.

OWLing at Different Stages

Children send messages in different ways as their communication develops. At each stage you need to **O**bserve, **W**ait and **L**isten carefully to what your child is "telling" you.

OWL with Discoverers

A Discoverer doesn't send messages to you intentionally. But when you observe her carefully, you'll get important clues about what she needs and what she's interested in.

A Discoverer who is very young or who has developmental or medical challenges goes through many stages of sleep and wakefulness during the day. These stages affect how ready she is to interact with you. By OWLing, you can tell when a Discoverer is most ready to interact. She may stop moving, or she may look toward you or smile. She may also move her arms and legs or make cooing or babbling sounds (especially when you're talking or singing to her).

A Discoverer will also let you know when she is *not* ready to interact – usually when she is hungry, tired or uncomfortable. If she's not ready to interact, she may look away, cry, fuss, squirm or frown. Then, she may need a break or she may need your help to calm down.

It's important to respond immediately when a Discoverer does something that seems to send a message. For example, she may make cooing sounds when she's feeling content. When you smile and coo back right away, you help her learn that cooing is a good way to get your attention. This helps her make the communication connection (see page 6) – the important step that takes her to the next stage of communication.

When she OWLs, Colin's mom sees that he's fascinated by his mobile.

OWL with Communicators

When your child starts sending messages *intentionally*, she has reached the Communicator stage. At this stage, she may communicate a lot, even though she doesn't use any real words yet. Remember to OWL: Observe her body language. Listen to her sounds. Wait to give her the time she needs to start an interaction. Then let her lead the communication.

Even though Megan's mom is busy buying groceries, she OWLs to give Megan a chance to show her the banana. Then she responds with interest.

OWL with First Words Users and Combiners

Even when your child can talk, you still need to OWL to encourage her to talk even more. Another reason to OWL with First Words Users and Combiners is that what they say can sometimes be hard to understand. But when you OWL, you can usually figure out what they mean.

Scott's mom wonders why Scott has said the word ball. *When she OWLs, she sees that he's pointing at the moon, which to him looks like a big round ball.*

Alicia's mom listens carefully. Then she understands that Alicia is asking her whether she has a hat.

Take the focus off getting your child to talk

Asking your child to say words for you doesn't really help her learn language. In fact, it can have the opposite effect because it takes the joy out of communication. Your child knows when you really want to communicate with her and when you just want to hear her say a word.

Pressuring Graham to talk makes him talk less. It also makes playing with the toy kitchen a lot less fun.

When Graham's mom takes the focus off talking, she lets Graham lead. Then he communicates because he has something he wants to say.

The desire to communicate comes from having something to say and knowing someone will listen. So instead of making your child repeat words after you, let her lead the communication and then follow her lead. If you need to remind yourself to take the pressure off, a good rule of thumb is "Don't say *say*."

Note that **"letting your child lead" doesn't mean letting her rule**. There are times when you should not let your child lead. For example, she may put something dangerous in her mouth or pour water on the floor. These are times for you to set limits, to say no and to help your child find another activity. The activities that will help your child learn language are the ones that allow the two of you to connect and have fun together.

Why Letting Your Child Lead May Not Be So Easy

Children's communication styles

Children have different styles of communicating. A child's communication style can either make it easier or harder for her to interact with others. A child's communication style depends largely on her ability to do two things:

- **start** interactions with others
- **respond** when others start an interaction with her

Communication style also has a lot to do with a child's personality, as well as how comfortable she feels in a situation. It can also be influenced by her language difficulties, as well as her physical health, side effects of medications and overall development.

There are four communication styles: Sociable, Reluctant, Passive and Own Agenda.

Sociable Communication Style: A child with a Sociable communication style often starts interactions with others and responds easily when others interact with her. A child who has language difficulties and a Sociable communication style may not use words, or may be hard to understand, but this doesn't stop her from trying to interact with others. She finds it easy to take the lead in an interaction.

Baby seep.

Alicia has a Sociable communication style and easily starts an interaction with her mother.

Reluctant Communication Style:
A child with a Reluctant communication style does not start an interaction very often. When she does, her message may not be obvious, and you may even miss the fact that she has communicated with you. A child with a Reluctant communication style finds it easier to *respond* to others than to start an interaction. She may need time to "warm up" before she'll respond, especially if she doesn't know a person well. Having communication difficulties may affect her confidence in her ability to interact with others.

Amanda has a Reluctant communication style. She responds to her dad when they play together, but she seldom starts an interaction.

It can be hard to connect with a child like Katie, who has a Passive communication style.

Passive Communication Style: A child with a Passive communication style rarely starts an interaction *or* responds. It's hard to connect with her because she appears to show little interest in people or objects. Children who are unwell or who take medications that make them tired may have a more Passive style than they would otherwise. Some children with developmental delays also have a Passive communication style.

Own Agenda Communication Style: A child with an Own Agenda communication style seems to tune others out and tends to play on her own. She seldom starts interactions with others. When she does, it's usually because she needs something. It can be hard to get a response from a child with this kind of communication style because she seems to be in her own world. She may play with one toy for long periods of time, or she may move quickly from one activity to the next, but she doesn't seem able to share her play with others.

Cameron has an Own Agenda communication style. Dad isn't sure how to get an interaction going with him because Cameron seems to prefer to play alone.

Take a moment to think about which communication style best describes your child *most of the time.* Children who have Passive, Reluctant or Own Agenda communication styles need extra support to get involved in an interaction. But even children with a Sociable communication style will benefit from your efforts to make interactions more successful, interesting and fun.

Parents' roles

Every day, as you and your child interact, you play a variety of roles. Many things influence these roles, such as your personality, your ideas about being a parent, your child's communication difficulties, her communication style and the challenges of a busy life. At one time or another, every parent takes on all of the roles described on the following pages, but playing certain roles too often can get in the way of your child's language learning.

Let's look at some typical parents' roles.

The Director Role: Parents direct their children's lives every day. They plan what their children will eat, what they will wear and when they will go to bed. But sometimes parents play the role of Director too often. They do most of the talking, telling their children what to do and how to do it. They may not realize that over-directing can get in the way of their child's learning. Children learn best when they lead interactions.

Robert wants to find the page with the monster, but his dad is playing the Director role, insisting that they read the book page by page.

When Brian's mom takes on the role of Tester, she's too busy asking questions to OWL and notice what has really captured his interest.

The Tester Role: Parents want their children to learn new skills. If a child isn't developing language as expected, her parents may think they need to work even harder to help her learn. So they take on the role of Tester, asking lots of questions to see what she's learned. But testing a child doesn't help her learn. A child learns best when she is having fun and her parents are tuned in to her interests.

The Entertainer Role: A parent in the Entertainer role is lots of fun and does whatever it takes to keep a child amused. The Entertainer tends to take the lead, doing most of the talking and playing. The problem is that the child doesn't have much opportunity to interact and be part of the fun. To learn language, children need to be actively involved in the interaction.

Scott enjoys watching his dad be the Entertainer but he doesn't have an opportunity to get involved.

The Helper Role: When a child has a hard time learning to communicate, her parents naturally want to make things easier for her. They tend to play the role of the Helper, doing everything for her and not expecting much communication. Parents of children with special needs may feel an even stronger need to play this role. But when parents are too quick to help, they may not find out how much their child can communicate and what really interests her.

> Uh-oh, do you want Mommy to get it for you?

When Sofía drops her toy, her mother becomes the Helper, rushing in to help before Sofía has a chance to do anything herself.

> It's six o'clock. We'd better hurry.

The Mover Role: Parents of young children are busy people, and their days are full of things to do. To stay on schedule, parents have to keep things moving fast. However, parents who play the Mover role too often may miss the chance to connect with their child and talk about things that interest her.

Megan's mom is in the Mover role because she is running late. She doesn't notice that Megan is trying to tell her something.

The Watcher Role: Sometimes parents would like to interact with their child but aren't sure how to join in. They may end up just watching her play or commenting on what she's doing from a distance. This is especially true if the child doesn't seem interested in interacting. Children do need some time to explore and learn on their own. But to learn language, they need to interact with their parents.

> You've got a mouse in your truck. That's a nice mouse. He wants some cheese.

In his role as Watcher, Cameron's dad does a play-by-play commentary from the sidelines.

The Tuned-In Parent

When it comes to helping your child interact and learn language, the most important role for you to play is the role of the **Tuned-In Parent** – tuned in to your child's interests, needs and abilities. Tuned-In Parents give their children opportunities to start an interaction, and then they respond immediately with interest.

You can't be a Tuned-In Parent all the time. But to play the Tuned-In Parent role more often, think about whether you are talking too much, asking too many questions, helping your child too often or rushing more than you need to.

When Robert's dad thought about it, he realized there was no reason to be the Director and to insist on reading every page in the book. So, he followed Robert's lead and let him turn to his favourite page with the picture of a monster.

Dad realizes that Robert is making a monster sound and follows Robert's lead. Now that he's the Tuned-In Parent, the fun begins.

Create Opportunities for Your Child to Lead

Sometimes OWLing isn't enough. If your child doesn't start an interaction with you – even when you're careful to wait for it – she may need more help from you. The following suggestions will help you create more opportunities for her to take the lead.

These ideas may not work right away. That may be frustrating for both of you, but it doesn't mean they won't work after a while. If you create an opportunity and your child doesn't take the lead, just show her what she could do or say and then carry on with the activity. She'll learn from your example, and next time she may start the interaction.

By putting his favourite toy out of reach, Miguel's mom creates an opportunity for him to ask for his teddy bear.

Help your child make a request

Instead of rushing to give your child something you know she'll want, create an opportunity for her to ask for it. Listed below are some ideas for helping your child make a request.

✦ **Place a Favourite Object out of Reach ... Then Wait:** When your child wants an object, place it in her view but out of her reach and then wait until she does something to ask for it. As soon as she asks for the object, give it to her.

✦ **Offer a Little Bit ... Then Wait:** Instead of giving your child a big piece of apple or a full cup of juice, give her a little bit, then *wait* for her to ask for more. As soon as she does, give her a little bit more, then wait again.

By giving Graham just a sip of juice, Dad creates an opportunity for Graham to ask for more.

✦ **Choose an Activity That Your Child Can't Do Without Your Help ...
Then Wait**: Children love bubbles, wind-up toys and musical toys.
Because your child needs your help to make these toys work, you can
use them to encourage her to lead the interaction. Instead of immediately
blowing the bubbles, winding up the toy or turning on the music, wait
to create an opportunity for your
child to ask for your help. When
she asks for help, give it to her.
But wind the toy up just a bit, or
blow just a few bubbles at a time.
That way you'll give her more
chances to ask you to do it again.

Again.

*After the wind-up toy stops, Dad waits,
creating an opportunity for Sofía to ask
him to wind it up again.*

✦ **Offer a Choice ... Then Wait**: It's easier
for a child to choose when you give her just
two choices.

*Jordan's mom creates an opportunity for him to
choose by reaching for the object he wants.*

✦ **Pause a Familiar Activity ... Then Wait**:
When you and your child are doing something
that can be repeated over and over – such as
playing Tickle, swinging on a swing or singing
a song – pause the activity from time to time.
Then your child can ask you to continue.

*When Dad stops bouncing Hanifa up and down,
she flaps her arms to tell him to keep going.*

Help your child make a comment or ask a question

No!

No, not on your hand. The shoe goes on your foot.

✦ **Change a Familiar Activity ... Then Wait:**
Instead of just pausing in the middle of a familiar activity or routine, you can also change it or leave out a step. The surprise creates an opportunity for your child to react and start an interaction by making a comment or asking you a question.

When Scott's dad does something wrong, Scott gets a chance to let him know he made a "mistake."

Hey ... car!

✦ **Hide Objects in Surprising Places ... Then Wait:** Let your child find a surprise to create an opportunity for him to tell you about it.

Brandon's mom has hidden a toy where Brandon will find it, creating an opportunity for him to tell her about the surprise.

✦ **When Things Go Wrong ... Wait:** Every day, little things go wrong. Spoons fall on the floor, crayons break and juice gets spilled. Instead of fixing these little problems right away, *wait* a few seconds to see what your child will do or say. You'll be creating an opportunity for her to send you a message.

Instead of picking up Robert's cookie immediately, his mom waits and watches him. Then Robert lets her know that his cookie has fallen on the floor.

Chapter 3

Follow Your Child's Lead

You and your child interact during daily activities like getting dressed, riding on the bus or playing in the park. These everyday activities create the best opportunities for language learning. The more your child takes the lead during these activities, the more you can respond by following his lead, which will build his confidence and communication skills. In this chapter you'll learn how to **follow your child's lead** to let the interaction grow.

Follow Your Child's Lead and Let the Interaction Grow

"Following your child's lead" means responding with interest to what your child is communicating to you. It means letting your child know that you've received his message and giving him the feeling that his message is interesting and important. It also means responding by building on what he has communicated.

There are many ways to follow your child's lead:

- respond immediately with interest
- join in and play
- follow your child's lead with your actions and words
  - imitate
  - interpret
  - make a comment
- follow through

Respond immediately with interest

When your child starts an interaction with you, respond *immediately*. If he sends you a message of any kind – a look, a sound, a smile, a body movement, a gesture or a word – do or say something right away to let him know you've received his message. Responding immediately with enthusiasm builds his confidence and encourages him to respond back to you. Children are attracted to a smiling face, and your smile is a wonderful way to show your child you're interested. Putting lots of animation in your voice helps, too.

When you respond, make sure you respond to what your child is interested in, not what *you* think is important. Ask yourself what he's thinking and feeling, then show him that you're interested in what interests *him*.

The reasons for following your child's interests are simple:

- he is more likely to communicate about what he's interested in
- he'll learn more when your response relates to his message
- it's very hard for him to switch his attention from what interests him to what interests you

If your child is a Discoverer, your quick response helps him understand that his movements and sounds mean something to you. This in turn helps him make the communication connection, when he realizes that what he does or says affects the people around him.

Mom responds enthusiastically to Sofía's message. This lets Sofía know that Mom is interested in whatever interests her.

Join in and play

Even if your child doesn't start an interaction with you, you can still get involved in what he's interested in. Join in and play with him. For example, if he's driving a toy car on the floor, join in. Get down on the floor with your own car and drive it near his, making car noises. Then watch the interaction grow!

Joining in the play is one of the best ways to follow your child's lead, creating all sorts of opportunities for fun and communication. To join in and play, first get face to face and OWL (observe, wait and listen) to see exactly how your child is playing with his toys. When you join in, play the way he's playing. Don't change the game. Remember to wait silently every now and again to give him opportunities to lead the interaction. Then follow his lead. Keep reading for some great ideas about how to join in and play.

"Join in and play" means adapting parents' roles

Do you remember the discussion about Parents' Roles in Chapter 2? If you find yourself overdoing the role of ...

- **Director** — get more involved in the play, but avoid taking over
- **Tester** — focus on playing and having fun instead of asking questions
- **Helper** — wait to give your child time to explore and discover on his own, rather than showing him how to play
- **Watcher** — get involved in the play by using toys to play like a child
- **Entertainer** — sit back and let your child lead the play, instead of putting the spotlight on yourself

Try to take on the role of **Tuned-In Parent** in play. Let your child play his way. Follow his lead and focus on playing together and having fun.

Play like a child

Can you remember how much fun it was to build a tower, play with toys in the bathtub, drive your toy cars or dress up your dolls? Look at toys and play activities through your child's eyes. Get down on the floor with him and have fun! Young children often play without a plan, so don't worry about what's going to happen next or if he's not playing the "right" way. Go with the flow, and stay with your child's interest.

Use fun sounds and words

Children enjoy sounds that are fun to hear and fun to make. Fun sounds and words are easy to remember and understand because they're said with lots of animation and often have gestures that go with them.

Use fun sounds and words that fit with what you're doing. If the two of you are going down a slide at the park, "Wheee!" is a fun word to say. If you're pretending to put a doll to sleep, say "Shhhhhh" and put your finger to your lips. When something goes wrong, saying "Uh-oh!" or "Woops!" while putting your hand up to your head always gets a child's attention.

Your child will probably love sounds that animals make, like "moo" or "meow," sounds that monsters or other characters make, like "Rrraahhr!" and sounds that vehicles make, like "Chugga-chugga, chugga-chugga!" for a train. Here are some other fun words that your child may enjoy:

- **Boom!** – when there's a big noise or something falls
- **Vroom-vroom! and Beep-beep!** – when he's playing with toy cars or trucks
- **Ouch!** – said with a pained look on your face as you touch the part of your body or your child's that hurts
- **Pssshhh!** – to make the sound of water running or pouring
- **Yuck! or Yucky!** – said with an exaggerated look of disgust
- **Yummy! or Mmmmm!** – while rubbing your belly
- **Bye-bye!** – when you wave
- **Peek!** – when you're playing a game of Peekaboo
- **Pop!** – when bubbles pop or when a toy, like a jack-in-the-box, pops up
- **Up! and Down!** – said with your voice going up at the end when you say *up,* and down at the end when you say *down*
- **Cheep-cheep! Woof! Oink!** and other sounds that animals make

Get your own toys

It's hard to join in and play when your child has the only toy. When that happens, you can easily find yourself in the role of Watcher. The solution is to get your own toy, one that is similar to your child's. For example, if your child is "driving" a toy truck or stacking blocks, find yourself something to drive or stack. Have an extra toy ready in case your child wants your toy or wants to have a toy in each of his hands.

Pretend

When children reach the First Words User and Combiner stages, they begin to pretend in their play. (Some Communicators who can understand far more language than they can express may also pretend in their play.) They make believe that toy objects are real, for example pretending to talk to Grandma on a toy telephone. (You'll learn more about pretend play in Chapter 7.) Pretending is a great way to join in the play. Take on a role, behave like the character you are pretending to be and make the play fun!

Mama.

Mama's gonna try some. Mmmm ... good soup!

The interaction is lots of fun when Graham pretends to feed his mom some soup and she pretends to eat it and enjoy it.

Follow your child's lead with your actions and words

When you follow your child's lead with your actions and words, you respond to what he says and does, letting him know you are listening. On the next three pages you'll find some strategies for letting the interaction grow in a gentle, natural way without putting the focus on getting your child to talk.

Imitate

One of the very best ways to connect with a young child who is just beginning to communicate is to imitate him by copying his actions, facial expressions, sounds and words. Start by getting face to face and OWLing to observe your child. Then do exactly what he does. If he bangs on his high chair tray, then you bang on something too. If he makes a sound, repeat his sound using the same rhythm, loudness and tone. If your child is a Discoverer or a Communicator, imitate any non-crying sound he makes — anywhere, any time.

Mom imitates Evan, saying exactly what he says. It's a great way to get the interaction going.

Let your child hear his words pronounced correctly

When children are learning to talk, there are many words that are hard for them to say. If your child says a word but mispronounces it, respond by repeating the word, but say it correctly. For example, if he points to the juice and says "Doos," respond by saying "Juice" (repeating it a few times). Then carry on with the interaction. There is no need to tell him he's not saying the word correctly or to ask him to say the word again. Let him experience success so that he feels encouraged, not self-conscious, about the way he is talking. Learning to pronounce words correctly takes a long time.

Interpret

Interpreting your child's message – putting into words what you think he is trying to tell you with his actions or sounds – is another powerful way to let him know that you are listening and trying to understand. Before you can interpret your child's message, first you need to OWL to understand what he's trying to tell you. For example, if your child reaches his arms out toward you when you enter his room, he's probably telling you he wants to be picked up, so as you lift him, say "Up!"

Interpret from your child's point of view. For example, if your child hands you his empty cup to ask for more juice, instead of saying "You want some more juice," say what *he* might say if he could: "Juice" or "More" or "More juice." When you interpret your child's message with just one or two simple words, he might imitate what you say right away. If not, hearing your example will help him know what to say when he's ready.

Robert kicks his legs to ask for a push. His dad interprets his message with one word, saying what Robert would say if he could.

Make a comment

Another way to follow your child's lead is to make a short comment that matches what your child is doing or saying at that very moment. A comment can be just one or two words or a short sentence. Use simple, clear language. Your comments can keep the interaction going by building on what your child is doing or saying, or by building on what he seems to be interested in. Comments also let you talk to your child about new and interesting things.

Scott's mom follows his lead with a comment.

Ask a question (but not too often)

Questions are a natural part of conversation. You can follow your child's lead by asking questions, but questions can make your child feel pressured. This is especially true if you ask too many questions or questions that have nothing to do with what he's interested in.

Questions will be discussed in more detail in Chapter 4. For now — unless your child is a Discoverer (see page 44) — avoid asking too many questions. The best ways to follow your child's lead are imitating, interpreting and making comments.

Combine responses when you follow your child's lead

When you follow your child's lead with your actions and words, you will often combine two types of responses. As a guideline, when you respond to your child — by imitating, interpreting, making a comment or asking a question — use no more than two of these responses at a time.

*Grace's mom combines two responses. First she **interprets** what she thinks Grace means. Then, she **makes a comment** about what Grace is doing.*

*Brian's mom **interprets** Brian's message, then **asks a question**.*

Follow through

When your child makes a request, it's important to follow through. For example, if he asks you to put on his shoe, follow his lead by imitating, interpreting or making a comment ... and then follow through by putting the shoe on.

Put your sock on. Mommy's gonna put your sock on.

Doh.

*When Cameron asks mom to put on his sock, she first interprets his message and then **follows through**, putting on his sock.*

Following through lets your child know that communicating can get him some of the things he wants. If your child asks for something you don't want him to have or can't give him, you can still follow his lead to let him know you've understood his message, then respond – as Graham's dad does.

Juice. That's enough juice. No more juice.

Doos.

Graham's dad can't follow through because Graham has had enough juice. But he still imitates Graham and then explains that there's no more juice.

Following Your Child's Lead at Different Stages

Follow the Discoverer's lead

OWLing with a Discoverer tells you a lot about how he feels and what he wants. Even though he doesn't communicate intentionally, you can respond to him as if he does.

Imitate: Imitate a Discoverer's body movements, actions and facial expressions. If he sticks out his tongue, stick out your tongue. Most importantly, imitate his sounds exactly the way he says them. If he says "Bah-bah-bah-bah," then you do the same. Imitate as often as you can. It creates a special connection. Your child may stop and look at you. If you wait, he may even imitate you back!

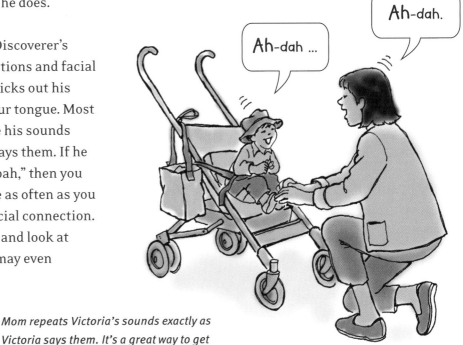

Mom repeats Victoria's sounds exactly as Victoria says them. It's a great way to get the interaction going.

Interpret: Interpret the Discoverer's movements, facial expressions and sounds *as if he were telling you something.* For example, if he smiles and makes a happy sound when you tickle him, think of this as his way of telling you he likes being tickled and say "Tickles. You like being tickled!" You don't need to keep your sentences short. Even though your child can't understand what you say, he loves to listen to the music in your voice, so keep it lively.

Here comes Andrew. Andrew wants to say hi.

When Dad notices that Katie is looking at her big brother, he follows Katie's lead by making a comment.

Make a Comment: Talk to a Discoverer *as if* he can talk to you. Comment often about what you're doing, what he's doing and what's happening around you. For example, if your child sneezes, you could say "Oh, that was a big sneeze!" If he hears the telephone ring, you could say "Phone. Maybe that's Grandpa! Grandpa's calling to tell you he's coming for dinner."

Ask a Question: For Discoverers, questions are a good way to stay connected. Even though your child doesn't understand your words, he loves the sound of your voice. When you ask a question, your tone changes, making you interesting to listen to. You can ask a Discoverer any kind of question. For example, if he looks toward a noise outside the room, you can ask "Did you hear a noise?" or "Did Daddy make a big noise?" If he yawns, you can ask "Is it time for your nap?" or "Are you getting tired?" The words you use aren't so important. What matters is that your child hears your voice and knows you're responding to him.

Join In and Play: Discoverers like to bang and shake toys and put toys in their mouths. When you join in and play with a Discoverer, you need to OWL so you know when he needs time to explore new things. To make it easier for him to look at you when he's holding a toy, get face to face. If you're showing him a toy, like a rattle, hold it close to your face.

Sometimes, you need to get your child's attention before he will look at a toy. To do this, do something interesting with the toy: shake it, move it around or touch him playfully with it. Move toys and objects slowly so that the movement or sound doesn't overwhelm him. To help your child change his focus from a toy to you, make fun, interesting sounds – such as clicking your tongue or gently calling your child's name. If your child looks at you even briefly, respond immediately with lots of enthusiasm by looking directly into his eyes, smiling and saying something – anything – to him.

When Jordan reaches for his teddy bear, Mom interprets his action as a request. To join in and play, she makes the bear dance.

Follow the Communicator's lead

Get face to face and observe the Communicator as he becomes interested in something. Wait for him to send you a message. Ask yourself "What's he thinking? What's he feeling?" so you'll be ready to follow his lead.

Early in this stage your child may still be learning how to share his thoughts with you. To do this, he has to look back and forth between you and what he's thinking about and point to it so you know what has caught his attention. To make it easier for him, position yourself next to the object, point to it or pick it up and hold it next to your face.

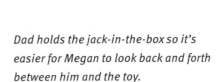

Dad holds the jack-in-the-box so it's easier for Megan to look back and forth between him and the toy.

Imitate: If you're not sure what to do, imitate! Communicators enjoy it when you imitate their actions, facial expressions and sounds. Do what your child does. Say what he says, using the same rhythm, loudness and tone. Imitate as often as you can. If your child repeats the action, imitate him again. Imitation can really get an interaction going, helping the two of you feel more connected.

Interpret: The Communicator sends specific messages using actions, looks, gestures, facial expressions and sounds. When your child communicates, decide what his message is and then interpret it. Put what you think your child means into *one or two words.* For example, if you give your child a piece of banana and he turns his head away or says "nuh-nuh," say the words that your child would say if he could: "No" or "No banana." Interpreting works the same way when your child is learning signs or picture pointing. Make a sign or point to a picture to interpret your child's message. *Always* say the word that goes with the sign or picture. Even though your child isn't saying words yet, interpreting his message teaches him something he can use when he's ready.

Mom interprets Hanifa's message by making the sign for cookie and saying the word at the same time.

Make a Comment: Make a comment that relates to your child's message or to what is happening at the moment. A comment can be one or two words or a short, simple sentence that your child can understand.

Join in and play with a Communicator by imitating what he does with his toys.

Join In and Play: A great way to join in and play with a Communicator is to imitate what he does with his toys. To do this, you'll need to get your own toys. If he's putting shapes in a shape sorter, join in and add your own shapes. If he's pouring water from a cup into a pail, get your own cup and pour water into his pail. While you play, use fun sounds and lots of animation in your voice to keep the interaction interesting.

Follow the First Words User's lead

Get face to face and start OWLing. Your child may send you a message right away, or you may need to give him time to start an interaction. When he sends a message and you're not sure what he means, ask yourself "What is he thinking? What is he feeling?" Remember to respond to his interests. Don't try to switch to something else.

Imitate: Imitate your First Words User's actions, sounds and words. Imitation continues to be a powerful strategy at this level and it can help keep the interaction going.

Imitate your child's word using the correct pronunciation.

Interpret: Interpret your child's gestures, sounds and words by re-expressing his message in one or two words. If your child uses signs or pictures to communicate, use one sign or picture combined with the spoken word to interpret his message. Remember to interpret from your child's point of view, saying the message the way he would if he could.

Interpret your First Words User's message with one word.
Hearing the word often will help him use it — when he's ready.

Make a Comment: Make a comment that relates to your child's message or to whatever is happening at the moment. A comment can be one or two words or a short sentence that your child can understand. For example, if he looks at an empty bowl and says "Gah," you could imitate his word by saying "Gone" and then add a comment, "You ate all your cereal!"

Join In and Play: Join in and play with a First Words User by playing like a child. Continue to use fun words and play with your own toys to make the interaction fun. Sometime during this stage, your child will begin to pretend, so join in and pretend along with him.

Follow the Combiner's lead

OWL until your child sends you a message. At this stage it's still important to get down to your child's physical level, but not necessarily face to face. There are some exceptions. If your child has a Reluctant or Passive communication style, being face to face will help you see his non-verbal messages and reassure him that you're listening to him. If your child has an Own Agenda communication style, getting face to face can encourage him to include you in an interaction. Being face to face has another advantage: if your child has a hard time pronouncing words, it allows him to see your mouth so he can observe how speech sounds are made.

Imitate: Imitate what a Combiner says by repeating his words, saying them correctly. Imitating actions is less useful with Combiners, but they still enjoy being imitated sometimes.

Make a Comment: Add a comment to what your child has said. At this stage, children can also talk about the past. For example, if your child talks about a storybook picture of a lion, you could add a comment about the lion he saw at the zoo.

Look, Daddy.

There's a butterfly on your sweater. Wow!

Laura's dad makes a comment to follow Laura's lead.

Join In and Play: Continue to pretend when you join in and play with your Combiner, taking on pretend roles. Your child will be delighted if you play the patient so he can be your doctor.

Brandon likes to pretend by playing doctor with Grandma. Even when he's looking in her mouth, Grandma remembers to interpret his message.

Following your child's lead by using the strategies you've learned in this chapter will help you to

- establish a connection with your child
- encourage his attempts to communicate and build his confidence
- give him more chances to participate in interactions with you
- create opportunities for language learning

Once you've followed your child's lead, remember to keep OWLing. Waiting will give your child an opportunity to respond to you and take the next turn in the interaction. You'll learn more about taking turns in Chapter 4.

Take Turns to Keep the Interaction Going

So far, you've learned how to let your child lead and how to follow her lead so the interaction can grow. In this chapter you'll learn how to help your child take turns so she can stay in the interaction longer. Helping your child stay in the interaction is important because the longer you keep an interaction going, the more opportunities she has to learn how to communicate.

Taking Turns at Different Stages

A turn looks different at each stage of communication. *Any* reaction by a Discoverer counts as a turn – a sound, a look, a smile, a slight movement or even a burp or a sneeze.

A Communicator has many different ways of taking a turn. She may look at you or use actions, gestures and sounds. Or she may use a combination of these. For example, if she wants to show you a dog she's seen, she may turn to look at you while pointing at the dog and making a sound. It's usually easy to notice a turn when your child uses her voice and makes a sound. Sometimes, however, Communicators take a turn without making any sound. If your child doesn't make many sounds, you'll have to observe her face, actions and gestures very carefully.

Jordan, a Discoverer, moves his arms and gives Mom a beautiful smile — and she treats this as his turn.

A First Words User's turns consist of single words – or signs or pictures – along with actions, gestures and sounds. The Combiner takes turns by combining two or three words, but she'll still use one word sometimes.

If your child has a Sociable communication style, she is probably already taking turns and having little conversations with you. If your child is a Discoverer or has a Passive, Reluctant or Own Agenda communication style, taking turns may not come easily. She may not know when or how to take her turn. If your child has a hard time taking turns with you, expect the conversation to be very short. By using the strategies described in this chapter, you'll learn how to help her take more turns with you.

Match Your Turns to Your Child's Turns

Your conversations with your child will be at their best when you balance them carefully. Having a balanced conversation means that you and she take an equal number of turns and your turns aren't much longer than hers. In other words, try to **match your turns** to your child's turns.

✦ **Match the Length of Your Child's Turn**: Your child's turns will be short. Try to match how much your child says or does by keeping your turns short and simple, too.

✦ **Match Your Child's Pace**: Let your child set the pace for the conversation. You may need to slow down and wait a little longer than you usually would to give her the time she needs to explore, understand or respond.

✦ **Match Your Child's Interest**: When you're having a conversation with your child, always focus on what she is interested in. She'll take more turns and stay in an interaction longer when you follow her lead.

Of course, having balanced conversations with your child starts with getting face to face with her and OWLing. By observing and listening, you'll know when she's ready to communicate and when her interest changes. By waiting, you'll give her the time she needs to send you a message once you've taken your turn.

In the illustrations below, Brian's mom OWLS and follows his lead. She matches her turns to Brian's, keeping her turns short and making sure that she and Brian take an equal number of turns.

1. Brian takes the lead – and the first turn – to let his mom know that his pants are dirty.

2. Mom follows Brian's lead, matching his interest by interpreting his message. She keeps her turn short. Then she waits.

3. With a word and a gesture, Brian takes his turn, telling his mom that she'll have to wash his pants.

4. Once again, Brian's mom matches his interest and keeps her turn simple and short. Then she waits for him to take his next turn.

Cue Your Child to Take a Turn

It takes children a long time to learn how to take turns in a conversation. A child may fail to take a turn simply because she doesn't realize that it's her turn. Even when she knows it's her turn, she may not know what to do or say, so she may do nothing.

The only way your child can learn to take turns is by interacting with someone who supports her and makes it easier for her. When parents are helping their children learn how to swim, they put water wings on them to help them float. In the same way, you can give your child **cues** to make taking turns easier until she can do it all by herself.

One of the best cues is the simple act of waiting. Waiting sends your child a clear message that your turn is over and that you expect her to take the next turn. But sometimes waiting isn't enough. Your child may need a cue that not only lets her know it's her turn but also shows her what kind of turn she could take. The cues discussed below can be used on their own or together with other cues.

✦ **Cue Your Child with Facial Expression and Body Language ... and Wait:** The look on your face and your body movements can signal your child that you're ready for her to take a turn. Here are some of the ways:

- Lean toward your child to let her know you're ready to listen.
- Open your eyes wide with anticipation and lift your eyebrows.
- Smile or nod your head to encourage her.
- Point to whatever has captured your child's interest.

Sometimes children learn to take turns just by responding to cues like these, especially if you wait for five to ten seconds. Without interrupting the flow of the conversation, these cues gently let your child know you expect her to take her turn. If your child responds to these cues, use them often, making sure she's looking at you before you try them.

Mom's facial expression and body language are cues for Katie to take a turn.

✦ **Give Your Child a Visual Helper ...
and Wait:** A visual helper is a cue that
your child can see. It could be an
object, a gesture, a sign or a picture. A young child learns best
when she hears *and* sees what
you're talking about. Visual
helpers give her lots of information to help her take her
turn. (You'll learn more about
visual helpers on pages 94-96.)

✦ **Pause or Change a
Familiar Routine ... and Wait:**
In Chapter 2 you learned how to
use a familiar activity or routine – such as swinging on a
swing or playing a game of Tickle
– to help your child start an interaction with you. During routines, your
child can learn a lot about how to
keep an interaction going, especially
if taking turns is new to her. To cue

*Tarik's Dad uses the toy as a visual helper
to cue Tarik to say its name.*

your child during a routine, pause with a look on your face that tells her
you're expecting her to take a turn before you continue. With a routine
that's very familiar, you can also change a few words or an action to surprise her and give her a chance to tell you that you've done something
wrong. (You'll learn more about using routines in Chapter 5.)

✦ **Give Hand-over-Hand Help ... and Wait:** Many of the games or songs
children enjoy include actions that your child can fill in to take a turn. For
example, during the song "If You're Happy and You Know It," your child
can clap her hands when you sing "clap your hands." Hand-over-hand help
shows your child exactly how to do a specific action. To teach her how to
clap, sing the song for her several times, clapping your hands as she
watches you. If after a few times she's still not imitating you, gently put
your hands over hers and show her what to do. Then continue singing
and show her again when you get to the next clap. After doing this many
times, pause the song before the claps and see if she claps on her own.

More.

Mom is helping Miguel learn how to make the sign for more *when he wants more bubbles. When he doesn't imitate her, she gently uses a hand-over-hand cue, saying the word* more *at the same time. Then she blows more bubbles.*

If not, help her hand-over-hand and keep singing.

Don't use hand-over-hand cues too often. They should be used only when your child understands the action and is close to being able to do it on her own.

✦ **Ask a Question ... and Wait**: Asking your child a question is another way to cue her to take her turn in the conversation. Ask only one question at a time, though, and wait to give her the time she needs to respond.

Remember that not all questions help your child take a turn. Some actually stop the conversation. Keep reading to learn more about different kinds of questions and which ones are best for your child.

What if my child doesn't take a turn?

Your child may need more time to learn when and how to take her turn. As a general guideline, follow her lead when you take your turn, and then wait. If she doesn't respond, cue her — using one or more of the cues described in this chapter — to let her know you're ready for her to take a turn. Then wait again.

If she still doesn't take a turn, take it for her. Do or say what she *could* do, keeping in mind her stage of communication. Don't pressure her to imitate your example. Just take your next turn and carry on with your conversation. This will keep the back-and-forth exchange going and avoid frustration for both of you. Make sure that your child is able to take the kind of turn you are expecting from her.

Ask Questions That Keep the Conversation Going

Asking and answering questions is an important part of communicating. Questions help you and your child understand each other's messages and thoughts. Questions also give you a way to follow your child's lead while cueing her to take the next turn. Let's look at some different kinds of questions so you can choose which ones are best for your child.

Choice questions

Choice questions let your child choose between two things – for example, "Want milk or juice?" These questions are the first ones she will be able to respond to, and so they create easy opportunities for her to take a turn. They also give her a feeling of control, which will encourage her to communicate more.

You can ask your child to choose between any two things – which hat she wants to wear, which toy she wants to play with or which book she wants to read. The easiest choice questions are the ones that involve real objects, so in the beginning it's a good idea to use visual helpers. Your child can then respond simply by pointing or looking toward what she wants. When your child can understand and say a number of words, you can ask choice questions without visual helpers. Always keep your questions short and simple. Obviously, when you ask your child choice questions, you should also be sure that either choice is acceptable to you.

Choice questions help prevent power struggles

While *It Takes Two to Talk* isn't a book about managing children's behaviour, choice questions can help you deal with the difficult moments that are part of life with a young child. For example, imagine you're out for a walk with your child. She doesn't want to sit in her stroller but she's tired of walking, so she sits down on the ground and refuses to move. You can avoid a power struggle by giving her two choices: "Do you want to walk...or take the stroller?" Use short sentences, slow down your speech, stress the important words and use visual cues, such as pointing to the stroller. Then wait for her to choose. If she doesn't make a choice, then you will have to make one for her. But at least you gave her the opportunity to choose.

Yes-or-no questions

Yes-or-no questions are questions that can be answered with a *yes* or a *no* – such as "Do you want to go outside?" or "Is Dolly thirsty?" This sort of question gives you a useful way of communicating with your child even before she can use words. Children learn to answer yes-or-no questions first by shaking their heads for *no*, then later by nodding for *yes*. You can also ask yes-or-no questions by saying words or phrases with a rising tone of voice at the end, as in "More?" and "All finished?"

WH– questions

WH– questions are questions that start with *what, who, where, when* or *why.* (Questions that start with *how* are usually also included in this group.) The first WH– questions that your child will be able to understand are short, simple ones that start with *what, where* and *who* – such as "What's that?" "Where's your teddy?" and "Who's at the door?" (Try to avoid testing your child by asking "What's that?" too often.)

Later, your child will understand questions that start with *why* and then, much later, questions that start with *when* and *how.* When and how questions are harder for your child to understand. To answer a when question, for example, your child needs to understand something about time. Questions that start with *when* and *how* should be avoided for now.

Avoid questions that stop the conversation

Asking your child a question can help her take a turn. But when questioning puts too much pressure on your child, it can also bring your conversation to a stop.

Graham's mom asks so many questions that Graham doesn't have a chance to take a turn – nor does he want to.

Conversation stoppers

Help your child stay in the conversation by
avoiding these conversation stoppers:

- asking too many questions
- asking questions that ...
  - your child doesn't have time to answer
  - test your child's knowledge
  - are too hard for your child to answer
  - don't have anything to do with what your child is interested in
  - answer themselves

Since it's obvious that Sofía has finished her breakfast, she doesn't need to answer the question.

Tarik has a lot to say, but his dad's yes-or-no question doesn't give him an opportunity to tell him all the things that are on his mind.

Asking Questions at Different Stages

You can ask your child choice questions, yes-or-no questions and WH–questions no matter what communication stage she is at. When you ask questions, remember to ask one at a time and to give her time to respond.

Questions for Discoverers

Even though a Discoverer can't understand your words, she likes to hear the sound of your voice when you ask questions, especially when you use lots of animation. Before asking a Discoverer a question, OWL to see what she's interested in. Then follow her lead by asking questions about whatever that is. For example, if she turns her head when she hears a loud noise, you could ask "What was that?" or "Did Ross drop his book?" If you notice that she's looking at the toy hanging over her crib, you could ask "Are you looking at your pig?"

Questions can be very interesting to a Discoverer if you exaggerate the tone and loudness of your voice. For this reason, you may want to repeat the question just to hold her attention. When you ask a question and wait with a smile and an encouraging look, your child may respond. She may take a turn by making a sound, changing her facial expression or wiggling her arms or legs. Her response may be subtle, but it's a turn.

You can also use choice questions with a Discoverer. Hold two real objects in front of her and ask which one she wants, and then wait for her reaction. Your child may look at the one she wants, or she may turn her head toward it or move toward it. Be sure that you hold the objects well apart from each other, so you'll be able to tell which one she's interested in.

Did the noise scare you? Was that a big noise?

Colin can't understand his mom's questions but the way they sound gets his attention.

Asking questions with Communicators, First Words Users and Combiners

If your child is a Communicator, a First Words User or a Combiner, keep these things in mind:

- Ask questions that your child understands.
- Ask questions that she can answer – with or without words.
- Ask questions that show her you're interested in what she's telling you.

Questions for Communicators

Ask a Communicator simple questions that she can answer without words – for example, with a gesture or a sound. Use visual helpers to help her understand your questions.

Choice Questions: Ask a Communicator choice questions using real objects, then OWL until she answers. She may look at, reach for or point to what she wants.

Yes-or-No Questions: These questions help a Communicator take a turn because she can answer by just nodding or shaking her head or by making a sound. Ask yes-or-no questions to find out what your child wants (for example, "Want to go outside?") or to help her tell a story ("And did the kitty run away?"). You can also use yes-or-no questions to clarify a message of hers that you're not sure you've understood.

When you and your child are involved in a familiar routine, you can ask a yes-or-no question to cue your child to take a turn. Pause during a routine or at the end of one and ask a question like "Want more?" or "Again?" Then wait for her to take a turn.

Do you want Cinderella or Pinocchio?

Hanifa, a Communicator, responds to Dad's choice question by pointing to the movie she wants to watch.

Adam looks up at the light to answer his mom's question.

WH– Questions: Some WH– questions can be answered without words. A Communicator can answer WH– questions that start with *what*, *where* or *who* by pointing or using a sound. For example, if you ask your child "Where's your sock?" she can hold up her sock. If she can't find it, she can hold her hands up to gesture "All gone."

Ask simple questions about objects and people that your child can see around her. This includes pictures in storybooks.

Questions like "What do you want to drink?" or "Who's that?" need to be answered with a specific word. Because Communicators don't use words yet, questions like these are conversation stoppers, so it's best to avoid them.

Questions for First Words Users

Questions give a First Words User a chance to use the words she can say. Before you ask a First Words User a question, be sure you've heard her use the word she needs to answer it.

Choice Questions: Once your child is a First Words User, you can ask her choice questions without visual helpers – if she can say both of the possible answers. If she can't say the names of the things she is choosing from, make sure she can see both objects (or pictures of them) so she can point.

Yes-or-No Questions: Asking a yes-or-no question is a useful way to check that you've understood a First Words User's message. It's also a way of helping her

Mom asks a yes-or-no question to check that she has understood what Scott is asking for.

take an easy turn to keep the conversation going. However, asking too many yes-or-no questions in one conversation may stop her from telling you what's on her mind.

Where are your shoes?

Dere!

Mom uses a WH– question to see if Brian knows where his shoes are.

WH– Questions: Ask simple what, who or where questions that your child can answer with a single word. For example, if you ask your child "Where's the birdie?" she could answer with a word like *there*, *sky* or *tree*. Of course, if she can see the bird, she could point to it instead.

When your child can't answer a WH– question, try a yes-or-no question instead. For example, if your child can't answer the question "Where are your shoes?" you could then ask "Are your shoes in your room?"

Questions for Combiners

Once children have reached the Combiner stage, they're usually able to answer questions about things they can't see around them. They may also be able to answer simple questions about something that happened earlier that day or something that is going to happen.

Choice Questions: When your child is able to combine two words, you can ask choice questions using short phrases, as Laura's mom does here.

Want to go to the park or go get ice cream?

Ice cream.

Mom's carefully worded choice question helps Laura answer it.

Yes-or-No Questions: As with First Words Users, asking a Combiner a yes-or-no question is a useful way to check that you've understood your child's message or to help her take an easy turn. However, if your child uses many different words and takes turns easily, questions that can be answered with a simple *yes* or *no* don't allow her to use all her language skills.

WH– Questions: You can ask a Combiner what, where or who questions as long as you know she has a way to answer them, with or without words. For example, a question like "What should we do?" can be answered by two-word combinations such as "Open door," "Make juice" or "Wash pants." Also, try to ask questions that encourage your child to think and to solve simple problems, such as "What happened?" or "Where can we find another one?"

Turn questions into comments

Many parents find themselves asking their children question after question in an effort to get a response. If you find yourself asking your child many questions, you're not alone. It's a natural reaction when your child has communication difficulties. But too many questions may turn your child off conversations. So, to limit the number of questions you ask your child, turn some of your questions into comments or statements.

Instead of a question ...	➤	try a comment
What's that? Is that a bird?	➤	Hello, bird!
That's a big truck, isn't it?	➤	It's a big truck.
Do you like that juice?	➤	Mmmm! Good juice.

Balance your questions with comments. Here's a general guideline: For every question you ask your child, try to make at least two comments.

Combine questions with comments

It takes children a while to learn how to respond to a comment. If your child doesn't respond to a comment, *combine a comment with a question.* For example, if your child sees a baby drinking milk from a bottle and says "Baby dink," you could say "The baby's drinking. What's the baby drinking?" Then she can take her turn and say "Milk."

Brandon's mom is careful to use more comments than questions in her conversation with him.

Turn-taking develops gradually, and big changes don't happen overnight. Be sure to keep it fun for both of you.

Chapter 5

Rewarding Routines

Think of all of the things you do with your child in an ordinary day. You get up, get dressed and have breakfast. Then you may take your child to daycare or preschool on your way to work. You may also go grocery shopping together or go for a walk to the playground. Of course, along the way there are more meals and snacks, diaper changes or toilet training, bath time and, finally, bedtime. You may have a song you always sing or a little game you always play at some of these times. Activities like these, which happen in almost the same way every day, are called **routines**. As you'll learn in this chapter, routines are a wonderful, fun way to introduce your child to taking turns and having conversations.

What Exactly Is a Routine?

All routines have four things in common:

- They have **specific steps**.
- The steps are always in the **same order**.
- They are **repeated many times**.
- People in the routine have **specific roles**.

Specific Steps: Routines are always made up of a series of steps. For example, a child's bedtime routine might consist of the following steps: put pajamas on, brush teeth, get into bed, read a story, kiss goodnight, turn out the light.

Same Order: Routines begin and end the same way each time, and the steps in between are always repeated in the same order. The words, sounds and gestures that are part of each step usually stay the same as well. Because the order of the steps in a routine is so predictable, your child soon learns to expect what comes next.

Repeated Many Times: As a routine is repeated over and over again, your child gets to know all the steps and the words, sounds and gestures that go with them. Once he knows a routine well, he relies less on you to guide him through it. He can then take more turns in the routine, and he learns exactly which turns to take and when.

Specific Roles: Each of you has a specific role to play in any routine, and each role involves specific actions. At first your child won't be able to play his role by himself. But with help from you, he'll begin to learn how. When he's older, he may become skilled enough take over *your* role. Then, he'll be the one to start the routine and the two of you will switch roles. (Role switching applies mainly to people games, described on the next page.)

The Many Routines in Your Child's Day

Every day, you and your child share many different kinds of routines. Some routines are a part of daily life in most families, and some may be unique to your family. Some of them are everyday routines — daily activities like changing diapers or going to bed. Others are little games that involve the two of you playing or singing together, which is why we call them people games.

People games

People games are play routines that involve just you and your child, without any toys. When it comes to people games, *you* are your child's favourite toy!

A few well-known people games are described below. You'll see that each of them has two simple roles, one for each of you. Later on in the chapter, you'll learn how to play them in ways that create more opportunities for your child to take turns.

Peekaboo
Children love the surprise when you disappear and then reappear in this game.

- Get face to face with your child, hold up a small blanket or towel and say "Let's play Peekaboo."
- Put the blanket or towel over your head and ask "Where's Mommy?" or "Where's Daddy?" You can ask this question a couple of times to hold your child's attention.
- Then, lift or pull the blanket off your head and look right into your child's eyes as you say "Peekaboo!" or "Boo!" Any simple words are fine, but use the same words each time so that your child learns to associate them with the routine.

As your child gets more familiar with the game, you can play another version of Peekaboo by peeking around a corner or from behind an object. When your child sees you, say "Peekaboo!" and then hide again in the same way. Wait a couple of seconds before you peek out again.

Hide and Seek

Help your child learn this game by finding a hiding place for him – under some pillows, under the bed sheets or behind a chair. Walk a few feet away from the hiding place so your child can't see you. Say "Where's (child's name)?" a few times. Then say, "One … two … three … Here I come!" and go and find your child. Pretend to look in a few other places first. Each time you look in a spot say, "Is (child's name) here?" When you don't find him there, say, "No, not here" or "Not behind the chair" to help him understand that you're looking for him. When you do find him, end the game by saying "There you are!" and giving him a hug.

When your child is first learning Peekaboo or Hide and Seek, it's important to keep the game moving quickly. If you take too long to find him, he might lose interest. As he becomes more familiar with the game, you'll be able to make the hiding part last a little longer.

Bouncy-Bouncy and Horsie Ride

Children enjoy the fun of being bounced up and down on your lap.

- Position your child on your lap so the two of you are face to face.
- Hold on to your child's hands or, if he needs more support, put your hands around him under his arms and bounce him up and down on your knees. You can bounce slower or faster, depending on what your child likes best. Say this rhyme while you're bouncing:

Bouncy, bouncy (*child's name*).
Bouncy, bouncy (*child's name*).
Up and down, up and down.
Bouncy, bouncy (*child's name*).

Later on, you and your child can play Horsie Ride by having him lie tummy down on your back, or by lifting him onto your shoulders.

Tickle

- Get face to face. Your child is usually lying on his back for this game.
- Hold your hands in a tickle position just in front of your child.
- Say, with lots of excitement and animation, "I'm gonna tickle you!"
- Then tickle your child in a playful way while saying "Tickle-tickle."

Gonna-Get-You, or Chase

This is a game in which you chase and catch your child.

- Get into position: If your child can walk, bend down a few feet away from him. If he sits or crawls, get down on your knees a few feet from him.
- Hold your arms up at shoulder level, with your palms facing out and fingers slightly bent as if you are going to grab him. Say "I'm gonna get you!" or "Here I come!"
- If your child is sitting or crawling, crawl slowly toward him, saying "I'm gonna get you!" as you crawl. If he is sitting, gently catch him, tickling him as you do. If he is crawling, gently catch him in your arms. If he is walking, then playfully run after him until you catch him in your arms.

- As soon as you catch your child, say "I got you!"

The high point of people games

People games are especially fun for children because they usually have a **high point,** or best moment. Often the high point occurs right at the end of the game. For example, the high point in a game of Chase is when you say "I got you!" The high point is what makes your child want to take a turn in the routine. High points can be so powerful that some children learn their first words from them.

Songs and rhymes

Children's songs and rhymes are another kind of routine that can help children learn to take turns. Some of these songs and rhymes, such as "The Wheels on the Bus," have actions that go along with them. "The Eensy Weensy Spider" (or "The Itsy Bitsy Spider") is sung with a finger play. Action-filled songs and rhymes like these are fun for your child and are also wonderful learning opportunities. Your child can learn to predict the gestures, words and sounds he's seen and heard so many times, and in time he might use them himself. (To learn more about songs and rhymes now, skip ahead to Chapter 9.)

Create your own routines

You can create routines just for you and your child. To do this, OWL to see what your child enjoys about an activity. Turn enjoyable moments into familiar routines by repeating them over and over again, making sure both of you take turns. Here are some examples of routines that parents have created:

The blowing routine always makes Jordan smile.

Blowing Routine: Jordan is a Discoverer, and his reactions are often just small body movements or slight changes in his facial expression. Jordan's mother noticed that he smiles when she blows gently on the side of his face, so she turned this into a routine the two of them can share.

Monster Noise Routine: Sofía is a Communicator. Her favourite book is *Where the Wild Things Are*. Each time her dad turns to a page that has a picture of the monsters, he makes a monster sound, which makes Sofía laugh. This moment has become the high point of reading the book.

Checking for Mail Routine: Robert is also a Communicator. His father noticed that he likes opening the mailbox to see if there is any mail inside. He also enjoys the squeaky sound it makes when he opens it. Now he and Robert check for mail together every day when they get home.

How Children Learn to Take Turns in Routines

Before your child can take turns in a routine, he needs to see and hear the routine again and again. This helps him learn all the steps and all the actions, words and sounds that go with them. Until he knows the routine well, you'll have to guide him through the steps.

As he becomes familiar with the routine, your child starts to participate in it by taking a turn. The easiest turn he can take is to ask you to repeat the routine when you have just finished it. He might also ask for the high point. Or, if you pause and give him a chance to take his turn, he might fill in an action, sound or word. For now, he still relies on you to help him play the game. Over time, he'll take more and more turns and he'll rely less on you.

Once Jamie knows the Peekaboo game, his mom sets up the routine and waits. He takes his turn ...

... and he's rewarded by his favourite part of the game.

Even later, your child may become so good at taking turns in his favourite routines that *he* may start the routine and even take on your role. For example, he may start the Peekaboo game by putting the blanket over your head, or even on his own head. Leading the interaction in this way is a very important step in learning to start conversations.

After playing Peekaboo dozens of times, Jamie can now start it, so he sets Mom up to play the game.

In time, Jamie learns to take on Mom's role. He puts the blanket over his own head and waits. When Mom says "Where's Jamie ?" he pulls the blanket off and says "Boo!"

Use a Routine to SPARK an Interaction

Choose a routine that's easy to repeat and that your child enjoys. It could be a people game, a song, a rhyme or a routine you've created. Once your child is familiar with the routine, you can use it to **SPARK** an interaction.

Start the same way each time.

Plan your child's turn.

Adjust the routine so your child can take his turn.

Repeat the same actions, sounds and words each time.

Keep the end the same.

Start the routine the same way each time

Give your routine a simple name. For instance, you could shorten a long name like "Ring Around the Rosie" to "Rosie." Then pick a visual helper to go with the name. For example, for Peekaboo, you could hold up the blanket when you say "Play Peekaboo?" Use this name and the visual helper each time you start the routine.

Want to play "Bunny"?

Over time, your child will learn to recognize the routine by its name and the visual helper. After a while he may ask for the routine by saying its name or by using the visual helper that you always use. Choice questions can give your child a way to request the routine before he's ready to do it all by himself. For example, you could ask "Want to sing 'Bunny' or 'Bus'?" to give him a choice between "Sleeping Bunnies" or "The Wheels on the Bus."

Brian's mom shortens the name of the rhyme "Sleeping Bunnies" to "Bunny" and hops like a bunny to start the routine.

Plan your child's turn

Plan *when* your child will take a turn

If your child is just beginning to take turns, you could set up the routine so that he takes his turn at one of these times:

- **at the end** of the routine, before you start again
- just **before the high point**
- **when you pause** during the routine

Up ...

Keri loves it when her dad lifts her high in the air.

... and down.

Again!

Dad planned that Keri would take her turn at the end of the routine when he brings her down again. So he says "and down" to let her know the game is over, and then he waits. Keri takes a turn by telling him "Again!"

Plan *how* your child can take his turn

What your child says or does to take his turn will depend on his communication stage and the situation. Here are some of the ways – based on the four stages – that your child could take a turn in the routine.

Discoverers: A Discoverer won't make a specific request for the routine to continue or to be repeated. But you can interpret any sign of excitement (such as faster breathing or kicking feet) or even the slightest reaction as a request for more.

Communicators: A Communicator takes a turn in a routine without using words. He may reach, point, make a sound or move his body. He may look at an object involved in the routine (for instance, a jar of bubbles) and then look back at you. He may even try to say a word that's part of the routine, like *Boo* for *Peekaboo*.

First Words Users: A First Words User can use a specific word or sign that is part of the routine, or he can point to a picture to take his turn.

Combiners: A Combiner can combine two or more words used in a routine, such as "fall down" or "We all fall down" from "Ring Around the Rosie." He can also use the word *more* with another word to ask for a routine to continue, as in "More 'Bunny.'"

Stir.

Stir ... You can stir the juice.

Graham, a First Words User, uses a single word to tell his mom what comes next in their juice-making routine.

Adjust the routine to give your child a chance to take a turn

You can adjust the routine by using cues to let your child know *when* to take a turn and *what* to do or say. Two of the easiest ways to cue your child are to pause the routine or change it. When you've just finished the routine, you can also use a word to cue your child to ask for more.

✦ **Pause the Routine:** Pausing the routine means stopping to give your child a chance to take a turn. Depending on his stage of communication, he could fill in a word or an action, or he could ask you to continue the routine or do it again. If a routine has a high point, the best time to pause the routine is just before it.

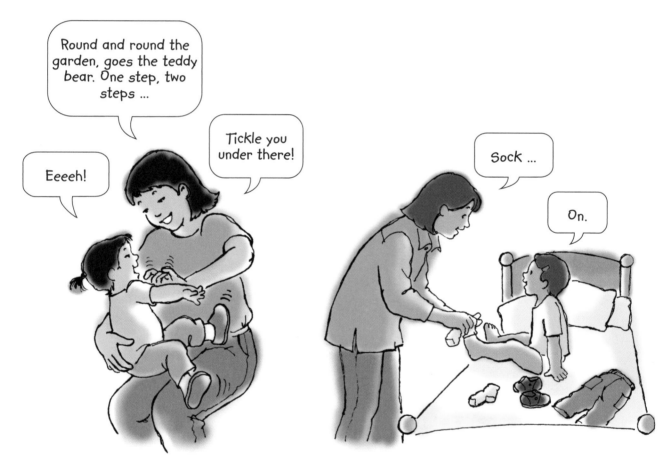

Victoria's mom pauses just before the tickling to let Victoria know it's her turn. When Victoria kicks her legs and makes a sound, her mom interprets this as a request to continue.

As Sofía gets dressed in the morning, her mom pauses to give her a chance to say the word *on,* which she has heard her Mom say every day for many months.

✦ **Change the Routine:** Change the routine to give your child an opportunity to tell you what is different or missing, what surprised him or what went wrong.

✦ **Use a Word to Cue Your Child to Ask for More:** To help your child ask for the routine to continue or be repeated, give him a cue by asking "More?" or "Again?" at the end of the routine. Be sure to use the same word each time.

Refer back to "Cue Your Child to Take a Turn" in Chapter 4 for more ideas on how to adjust the routine. If your child doesn't take a turn even after you give him a cue and wait, take his turn for him by doing or saying what you think he could do. Then continue with the routine. Each time you do this he'll learn from your example.

When Dad changes the checking-for-mail routine, Robert takes a turn to let his dad know that he sees the surprise in the mailbox.

Repeat the same actions, sounds and words

Think of your routine as a series of steps, and follow them in the same order each time. This will make it easier for your child to learn the routine, so he'll know what's going to happen next. As you follow the steps, always use the same words, sounds and gestures. For example, when you're playing Peekaboo, decide what you'll say when you take the blanket off — and say that word every time. Changing what you say from "Peekaboo!" to "Here I am!" will make it harder for your child to learn the routine.

Keep the end the same

Your child needs to know when the routine has ended. Keep the ending the same each time you finish. The end of a bedtime routine might be turning out the light and saying "Night night!" The end of a routine for getting in the car might be buckling your child's seat belt and saying "Click." If a routine (such as swinging on the swing) doesn't have an obvious end, you could say something like "All done" or "Finished."

Follow your child's lead ... wherever it goes

Routines are fun, but your child may not always be in the mood for the routine you've started. Don't worry about it! If something outside the routine interests your child, be ready to stop the routine and follow his lead.

Chapter 6

Add Language to the Interaction

As part of following your child's lead, you're already adding language to your conversations with her. In this chapter, you'll learn how to add language in ways that will help your child understand her world better and express what's on her mind. You'll also learn how to set communication goals to help your child take a better turn or move on to the next stage of communication.

First Experience, Then Understanding, Then Words

Parents look forward to the day their child uses her first words or signs. But many important steps lead up to that day. A child's earliest learning takes place through her **experiences** – what she sees, hears, touches, tastes and smells. During these everyday experiences, she hears you say the same words again and again and starts to figure out what they mean. Soon, she points to her nose when you ask "Where's your nose?" and follows simple instructions like "Give the book to Daddy." This is the beginning of **understanding**. Your child has unlocked the door to language!

Once your child understands many words, she may be ready to start saying some of them. She may imitate a word when she hears it, or she may use it on her own. She may not be able to pronounce words correctly. She may say "dop" for *stop*, "nana" for *banana* or "no" for *nose*. Or she may say something that doesn't sound like the real word at all. For example, she may say "baba" for *blanket* or "ugah" for *music*. You'll know what her word means because she'll use it the same way every time.

Learning to talk takes time. It can be frustrating or discouraging if a child doesn't use words or signs. Be patient. Your child may need to hear a word many, many times before she'll try to say it. If she doesn't try to say words, it may be because she is not yet ready or able to. But even if she isn't saying words, she is still learning what they mean, and that's an important step on the road to language.

Signs and pictures can help

If your child is having a hard time learning to say words, a speech-language professional may suggest teaching her to use signs or point to pictures. Using signs or pictures won't interfere with your child's ability to learn to speak. In fact, it will actually help her understand and learn words. Signs and pictures can also make her less frustrated because they give her a way to express herself. In other words, they can be stepping stones to words.

The more times your child sees you make a sign or point to a picture, the easier it is for her to make the connection to what it means. When your child has seen you use a sign or a picture many times, she may be ready to try these herself. Like first words, early signs may be simpler versions of adult signs that are easier for your child's hands to make.

Add Language All Day Long

Adding language is a natural part of your day. Rather than setting aside special times to teach your child to talk, take advantage of the time you already spend together. Build language learning into everyday routines and activities and turn any time you share with your child into a time for communication.

Add language during routines: Robert's dad says "Ready, set ... go!" each time he is about to push Robert on the swing.

Add language during daily activities: Laura and her Mom water the plants every day. When Laura says "All gone" her Mom responds by adding information about what Laura is most interested in — her watering can is empty.

Add language when something unusual happens: When the juice spills, Jamie's mom gives Jamie the words to describe what has happened.

Add Language to Build Your Child's Understanding of the World

Children have a lot to learn about the world, and they learn much of it through language. First, children need to understand what words mean. Part of learning about words is learning how one word can describe many things. For example, *bottle* describes containers of many shapes and sizes. Children also have to learn many things that we as adults take for granted – what is going to happen in the future, why people do the things they do, how objects are the same or different and many other things.

From the time your child's understanding is at the Communicator stage, she's learning all these things from interacting with you and hearing you talk about them. When you add language, you introduce her not just to new words but also to new ideas. She may not understand what all your words mean, but that's okay. With your help and with lots of repetition, she'll come to understand them and, in time, use them herself.

Refer back to the checklist on pages 11–13. Are your child's understanding and expression at the same stage? If her understanding is at a more advanced stage, keeping this in mind will help you add language in ways that will develop both parts of her communication.

Communicator or First Words User Stage of Understanding: If your child's understanding is at the Communicator or First Words User stage, most of the language you add will be about what is happening *right now*. You'll talk about the doggie going "woof-woof," children playing ball outside, lights going on and off – all the things that she is seeing and hearing.

Children whose understanding is at one of these stages also need to hear you talk about things that are *not* happening now. Start by talking about familiar things that will happen in the very near future. Use short, simple sentences.

Robert is just starting to learn all about airplanes from his dad.

For example, when you are undressing your child for her bath, you could point to the water running into the bathtub and say "You're going to have a *bath*." You can also talk about events that have just happened. A minute after Grandma leaves, for instance, you could say (waving as you say it), "Grandma's gone. Grandma said bye-bye." Start giving simple explanations for *why* things happen, such as "Baby's crying. Baby wants a bottle" (making a sucking sound). Repeat these ideas often, adding gestures and facial expressions to help her understand. In this way, you start exposing your child to language that will build her understanding of what's going on in her world. She may not understand everything you say, but in time her understanding of words and of the world will grow.

Combiner Stage of Understanding: As your child's understanding reaches farther into the future and the past, she begins to understand sentences like "You're going to Katie's birthday party tomorrow" and "We saw Jesse at the park." Now that you are adding language to build her understanding of more complex ideas, your sentences will grow longer. At this stage of understanding, you can add information and ideas that encourage your child to pretend and imagine, talk about her feelings and past experiences, and solve problems.

Dad adds language by explaining to Cameron why his truck won't fit into the hole.

Add Language to Help Your Child Express Herself

The way you add language to help your child express herself depends on her stage of communication development. At each stage, your child will need something a little different from you.

Talk to a Discoverer as if she can talk to you

When you add language with a Discoverer, talk to her as if she can talk to you. First OWL to find out what has captured her attention. Then look right into her eyes and talk about it. Be enthusiastic and animated and use fun sounds and gestures. If you find yourself repeating what you say again and again, just keep on repeating. It's all part of talking to a Discoverer and holding her attention. If your child is quiet and doesn't interact easily, don't become quiet yourself! Your child needs to hear your voice whenever you are with her. The more your child hears your voice, the more she'll discover and use her own.

Dad sees that Katie has noticed her brother, so he adds the words that describe what has captured Katie's interest.

Help Communicators, First Words Users and Combiners express themselves

> When you add language to help a Communicator, a First Words User or a Combiner to express herself, keep these important strategies in mind:
>
> - Give your child a word
> - Use a variety of words
> - Expand your child's message

Give your child a word (or a sign or a picture)

When your child communicates with you, follow her lead and respond by giving her a word or a few words that capture what she's telling you. Keep your responses short, but keep them grammatical. Giving her a word or a few words shows that you are interested and understand her. Some of the words you give her may be new words or words she understands but can't say yet. Remember that it's not enough for your child to hear a word once or twice. She'll need to hear a word again and again before she can remember it and, eventually, say it herself. During one interaction, try to repeat a word about **five times** so your child can remember it and eventually be able to say it. Count the number of times Dad says *phone* during his interaction with Grace below.

Grace gives Dad the phone, so he gives her the word for it — and repeats it three times.

Grace is still very interested in the phone so Dad says the word again and again to help Grace learn it.

Match Your Words to What's Happening at the Moment: Whether your child is communicating directly to you or is doing something on her own, it's important to add language by giving her a word or two. If she's playing or attending to something and isn't communicating directly to you, give her a few words that describe what she's doing, what she's looking at or listening to, and what she might be thinking or feeling. Match your words to what's happening **at the moment**. This makes it easier for your child to learn a new word. For example, if you see her looking at someone's glasses and you say *glasses* right away, she can connect the word to what she sees.

Rain. It's raining!

Sofía's attention has switched from the raisins to the rain outside, so Mom gives her a few words, matching them to Sofía's new interest.

Use the Same Word for the Same Thing Each Time: When adding language and giving your child words, always use the **same word** for the same thing. For example, if you refer to a cat as "cat," don't change this to "kitty" or "kitty-cat." It will be much harder for your child to learn any of these words if you do.

Use Specific Words with Your Child: Make a special effort to use **specific words** rather than words like *it*, *that* and *them*, which don't help children learn new vocabulary. Try to use the actual words you want your child to learn — and use them again and again. For example, if you give your child a spoon to put on the table, instead of saying "Here's a spoon. Put *it* on the table," say the word *spoon* each time: "Here's a spoon. Put the *spoon* on the table."

Use a variety of words

When you're helping your child express herself, it's natural to tell her the names of things, for instance *dog*, *book* or *ice cream*. But your child needs to learn many other kinds of words. Look at all the words you can use to talk to your child about a teddy bear.

Names:
bear, teddy

Question words:
what, where

Words that describe:
soft, big, all gone

Words that express belonging:
my, Mommy's

Action words:
sleep, eat, hug

Social words:
night-night, bye-bye

Words for feelings:
happy, sad, tired

Location words (where things are):
up, down, under

Which words should you add for your child? Start with words for the things your child is most interested in — words she understands and communicates about through actions or gestures but can't yet say or sign. Think about the words your child would want to say. For example, you might want her to learn the word *potty*, but she may not care about that word at all. Maybe she'd rather say *doggie*, *ice cream* or *on* (for a light) because those things really interest her.

Once your child uses about 50 words or signs, she may be ready to combine words into two-word sentences. When you add a variety of words, you give her the building blocks she needs to do this. Action words like *push*, *jump* and *sleep* are especially important because they combine easily with other words to make two-word sentences (such as "Daddy sleep" or "Push truck").

Knowing a variety of words gives Brian the building blocks he needs to combine words.

Expand your child's message

Whether your child uses just one word at a time or two or more, you can help her speak in longer sentences by expanding her message. Do this by responding with a slightly longer sentence, always including her words to make the sentence more complete. Even if she can understand longer sentences, keep your sentences short, but grammatical. This is how you help her build her ability to express herself.

Mom expands Scott's message, adding a few words to the word he said.

On.

Okay, let's turn the water on!

Mommy apple.

Mommy's eating the apple.

Brandon's mom expands his message to show him the next step, using an action word.

Highlight your language

Helping your child understand and use language is a bit like playing a game of catch with her. You do everything you can to help her catch the ball. You use a larger, softer ball. You get her attention. And then you gently toss, roll or give the ball to her. You wouldn't think of throwing the ball hard or throwing it when she isn't looking.

It works the same way when you talk to your child. In other words, it's not just *what* you say to your child that helps her learn language, but *how* you say it. Making the words that you add stand out – **highlighting** them – helps her understand them and, in time, learn to say them.

To highlight the words you are adding, use "The Four S's:"

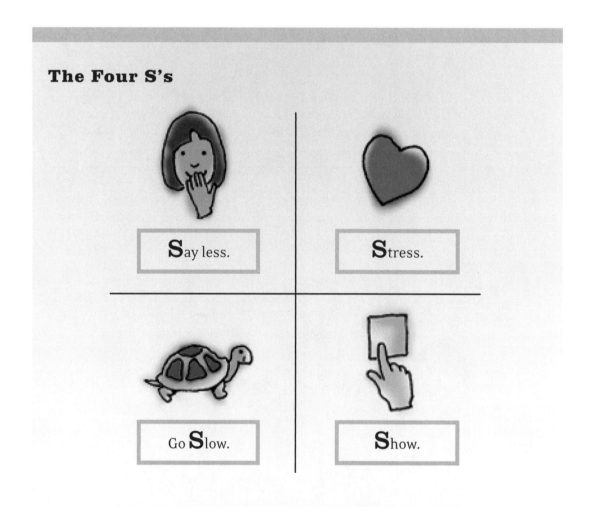

The Four S's

| **S**ay less. | **S**tress. |
| Go **S**low. | **S**how. |

Then *Repeat, Repeat, Repeat.*

✦ **Say Less:** Use short, simple but grammatical sentences when you talk to your child. She can't take in a lot of information all at once. When you say less, it's easier for her to understand and remember the words you use. It's also easier for her to imitate a word when it is highlighted in a shorter sentence.

Dad's one sentence has 18 words — too much information for Sofía to understand.

Short, simple sentences make it much easier for Sofía to understand what her dad is saying.

✦ **Stress:** Make important words stand out. For example, in the sentence "This tea is very hot," the most important words are *tea* and *hot*. Stressing these words gets your child's attention and helps her understand and learn them. It also makes it easier for her to try to say them. To put stress on words, use lots of animation in your voice, say the words a little louder or change your tone of voice.

Megan's Mom stresses the important words to make them stand out.

✦ **Go Slow:** Slow down your speech when you talk with your child to give her time to understand what you're saying. You'll also be giving her a chance to try saying a word herself. Some words, such as *open,* can be stretched out and said more slowly: "O-o-o-open." You can also pause slightly between your words.

✦ **Show:** Young children learn language best when they can see what you're talking about. **Visual helpers** provide many ways to show what a word means. Once you understand the different ways of using them, you can decide which visual helpers work best for your child.

There are three basic ways to use visual helpers: **showing or pointing** to what you're talking about; **adding actions, gestures or signs** to your words; and **using pictures** of the things you're talking about.

Show or point to what you're talking about: Showing or pointing to things helps your child in two ways. If *you* are talking, then it helps her understand what *you* are talking about. If *your child* is sending a message, point to what *she* is talking about. This will let her know that you're listening and that you understand what she's saying.

Visual helpers, such as pointing, help your child make the connection between the words you say and what they mean.

Add actions, gestures or signs to your words: Using actions, gestures and signs when you talk will help you "show" your child what you're saying. For example, you can shake your head when you say "No," put your arms up when you say "Want up?" and wave when you say "Bye-bye." This will help your child understand your words. But it will also show her a way of communicating without words, which she may learn to use herself.

Dad's gesture helps Jordan understand what's going to happen next and gives him a chance to take a turn.

When Mom interprets Hanifa's request, she adds the sign for cookie to the word.

Use pictures of the things you are talking about: Showing or pointing to pictures can help your child understand what you're talking about when the real objects aren't in sight.

Robert isn't sure what his mother is saying ...

... until she shows him a picture of what she's talking about.

Some pictures are easier for your child to understand than others. If your child is still learning to recognize pictures, use photographs or lifelike colour pictures. Show her pictures of objects and people that are important to her. Talk about the pictures in her favourite books. And put pictures beside real objects.

Use pictures to keep your conversation going, not to test what your child knows. Rather than asking her "What's that?" when you look at a picture, show her the picture and then wait to see what she says or does. Then follow her lead, respond and give her an opportunity to take another turn.

✦ **Repeat, Repeat, Repeat:** Repeat new words often and in different situations. The more often your child hears a word (or sees a sign or picture), the more easily she'll understand and remember what it means – and the more likely she'll try to say it. Repeat words several times in one turn. Then wait and let your child take a turn, and then repeat the word again. You can also repeat a word by combining it with a variety of other words, as in "Take your sock *off*" ... "Take your shoe *off*" ... "Take your pants *off*." Repeat words in different situations too. For example, use the word "off" in other situations (as in "Turn the light off" or "Turn the water off"). Don't insist that your child repeat the word back to you. Of course, it's great if she's ready to say it on her own.

Add Language in Two Ways

So far you've learned about two ways to add language: to build your child's understanding of the world and to help her express herself. In reality, very often you'll combine these two ways in one turn, as in these examples:

> Truck. ...You found your truck!

*Robert is a Communicator. His dad adds language in two ways for him by **giving him a word** (to help him express himself) and then **describing what's happening** (to build Robert's understanding of the world).*

> Heavy. ... That bag has the potatoes in it. Potatoes are heavy."

> Uh!

*Scott's mom adds language in two ways for Scott, a First Words User. She **gives him the word** heavy so he can learn to say this instead of uh. Then she gives him a **simple explanation** that builds his understanding.*

> The baby's sleeping. ... We need to be quiet so we don't wake her up.

> Baby seep.

*Alicia is a Combiner. Her mom **expands** her two-word sentence into a more grammatical three-word sentence. Then she **adds an idea** to develop Alicia's ability to imagine.*

Children with More Than One Language

Today, many families speak more than one language at home. Many others use one language at home and another one outside the home. If the members of your family speak two or more languages, you may wonder which one you should use when you talk to your child. It is very important for a young child to learn her first language well, since she will learn a second language more easily when the first one has a strong foundation. Your choice about which language to use with your child will depend on many things, including your attachment to your first language and your fluency in and comfort with your second language.

If you want your child to learn more than one language, be as consistent as possible in your approach. There are two basic ones:

✦ **One Person, One Language:** In this approach, you decide which person will speak which language to your child – and you stick to it. For example, you might speak to your child in English all of the time, and her grandmother might always speak to her in another language. If you decide to do this, you should not mix languages. Your child should know which language to expect when she is communicating with an important person in her life. If she hears the same person switch back and forth between two different languages, it will be confusing for her.

✦ **One Location, One Language:** In this approach, your child learns one language in one place and a second language in a different setting. For example, you may use one language with your child at home and she may learn another language at daycare or preschool.

Beso.

Mom talks to Miguel only in Spanish at home. He learns English when he goes to preschool.

It can be helpful to talk to a speech-language professional if you are concerned about which language to speak to your child, especially if she has a severe communication delay. However, remember that your child will learn language best when you communicate with her in a language that feels natural and comfortable for *you*.

Choosing Communication Goals

Look back to the checklist at the end of Chapter 1. The behaviours that you checked off under "Expression" describe how and why your child communicates. They are also what your child does or says right now to take her turn. This is the starting point for choosing communication goals to help her express herself better. (In Chapters 7 and 8 you'll learn how to set goals to increase her understanding, too.)

Until now, you've accepted almost anything your child does as a turn. Your next step is to help her take *better* turns. There are two basic ways to do this. You can help her do more of the things that she's doing now at her stage of communication development. Or, if she's ready, you can help her take a step toward the next stage.

Helping her do *more* of what she's doing now means helping her to:

- imitate or use more sounds
- imitate or use more gestures
- imitate or use more single words and a
  wider variety of words (such as action words)
- use more two- or three-word sentences

Helping her take a step toward the *next* stage means helping her to:

- turn an action into a gesture
- turn a word she understands (but doesn't say) into a gesture or word
  she tries to imitate
- turn an action or gesture into a word she tries to imitate
- turn a single word into a two-word sentence
- turn a two-word sentence into a three-word sentence

When can you say that your child "has" a word?

First, your child will **imitate** a word, saying it only when she hears you say it. Her imitation may sound nothing like the real word, but in her mind, she is saying the word. Some children imitate words for a very long time. Eventually, your child may say the word all by herself. You can assume that your child "has" a word when she says it **at least three times in three different situations** without hearing it first.

When choosing communication goals for your child, remember to make sure they are useful, specific and realistic.

✦ **Useful:** The goal for what your child will do or say to take her turn should make it easier for her to ask for what she needs and express what she really wants to tell you. Make sure you choose goals that *your child* will want to express, rather than what you think she should say.

✦ **Specific:** Communication goals should be specific enough for you to know when they've been achieved. Here's an example of a specific goal: "My child will try to say *on* to ask me to turn the water on at bath time."

✦ **Realistic:** Choose goals that are realistic, based on your child's communication stage and abilities. Don't expect too much too soon. Your child will not be able to go from using a gesture to saying a word all by herself. She may imitate the word for a long time first.

Choose communication goals that are "in the zone"

Communication goals that are "in the zone" are based on what your child is ready – with your help – to do or say to take her turn. For example, if your child says only a few words, it's unrealistic to expect her to put words together to make two-word sentences. However, she should be able to learn some new words. Help your child communicate successfully by choosing communication goals that are within her reach – neither too easy nor too difficult. Use the checklist at the end of Chapter 1 as a guide for what she might say or do next to take her turn. Look at the "Ideas for Choosing Goals" at the end of this chapter for more ideas. If possible, follow the advice of a speech-language professional.

Example 1: Turning a gesture or action into a word the child tries to imitate

Robert is a Communicator with a Reluctant communication style. He communicates through a combination of looking, actions, gestures and some sounds. However, he usually makes requests using actions and gestures. For example, when he is on the swing and wants his dad to push him, he rocks back and forth. Dad has recently heard him use sounds that are actually his first attempts at words, especially during people games. So Dad thinks Robert can learn to imitate a word, even if it is just one sound in the word.

Goal: "After Dad says 'Go!' Robert will take a turn by imitating the word 'Go!' (or making any sound that stands for it) to request a push on the swing."

✔ **Useful:** Robert loves the swing, so he will want to make this request.
✔ **Specific:** Robert's father will know when Robert has achieved this goal.
✔ **Realistic:** Robert uses sounds like "Boo" for Peekaboo and "Buh" for Bouncy-Bouncy in people games. Therefore, this is a goal that is in the zone for Robert.

To help Robert achieve this goal, his dad does these things:

- He starts by putting Robert in the swing and saying "Ready, set ... " and then waiting for Robert to request a push. Robert does what he has always done – rocks back and forth. But this time, Dad doesn't push the swing. He says "Go!" as soon as Robert rocks back and forth. Robert rocks again and Dad says "Go!" again, making sure he says it while Robert is rocking so Robert realizes this word is another way of making this request.
- Dad waits and cues Robert to say the word *go* by leaning toward him with an expectant look on his face – smiling, eyes wide and eyebrows raised.
- He repeats "Go!" when Robert continues to rock, and then he waits again. This time Robert gets the message and says "Oh." Dad says "Go!" and immediately pushes the swing – but not too hard, so it will slow down soon and he can try it again!

- Dad repeats this sequence again and again. He always says "Go!" when Robert rocks the swing because Robert needs to know that "Go!" is sending the same message as the rocking. Soon Robert will realize that rocking back and forth isn't working. He'll wait for Dad to say "Go!" and then he'll imitate the word, saying "Oh."
- After Robert imitates *go* many, many times, Dad will say, "Ready, set ... " and then wait to see if Robert is able to say "Oh" for *go* without hearing Dad say it. But that can take time and shouldn't be expected for now.

Learning to communicate takes time and patience. If Robert doesn't try to say *go* to request a push on the swing, Dad could give him some more cues. He could gently jiggle the swing and repeat "Ready, set ..." and "Go!" While Dad should already be face to face with Robert, he might need to move even closer to make it as easy as possible for Robert to look at him. If, even after extra cues, Robert still doesn't take a turn, Dad should keep the routine going and try again a little later. Robert may need more experience with the steps in the routine so that he knows that the words "Ready, set ..." are a cue for him to take his turn and make a sound that stands for *go*.

Robert is used to Dad pushing the swing when he requests it by rocking back and forth. But today, Dad says "Go!" and waits. This tells Robert that his dad expects him to try and imitate the word. It works! Robert takes a turn by imitating Dad with the sound "Oh."

Example 2: Learning to say an action word (to increase the variety of words)

Sofía is a First Words User who uses a number of single words as well as many gestures. She says words like "baba" for *bottle*, *up*, *doggie*, *mama* and *dada*, but she uses very few action words.

Goal: "Sofía will use the word *open* when asking her Mom to open the bubbles bottle, a bag of cookies, the door, the mailbox, the large container with her farm animals etc."

- ✔ **Useful**: There are many, many things Sofía asks her Mom to open, so Mom knows she is motivated to use this word.
- ✔ **Specific**: Mom will know when Sofía has achieved this goal.
- ✔ **Realistic**: Sofía is already using single words including two action words, so this goal is in the zone for her.

To help Sofía achieve this goal, her Mom takes these steps:

- She thinks of all the situations in which Sofía asks her to open something and decides to use these opportunities to help Sofía learn to say the word *open*.
- She makes sure she and Sofía are face to face every time Sofía wants something opened. When Sofía asks Mom to open something by handing it to her or touching it, as well as by looking at Mom and making a sound, Mom says "O-o-open" a few times, slowly and loudly (highlighting the word).
- Then she waits, with an expectant look on her face, keeping her mouth in the shape of the O sound to cue Sofía. She holds onto the bottle, bag or door that Sofía wants opened, but she doesn't open it.
- She repeats the word "O-o-open" once or twice if Sofía grabs the bag or pulls on the door.
- As soon as Sofía tries to say the word, even if she just says part of the word, Mom says "Open" and opens the bag, bottle or door.

If Sofía doesn't try to say the word *Open* after a few tries, Mom says "O-o-open" and then opens whatever it is that Sofía wants opened.

To help Sofía learn the action word open, *Mom says the word for her before she opens the chocolate bar. Sofía imitates the word and gets the chocolate.*

Once your child has shown that she can take a better turn, then it's important to encourage her to use what she has learned. When you're *absolutely certain* that she can take her turn in a new way, then let her know that you now expect it. If she doesn't use a word when you know she can, for example, wait a little longer, encouraging her with a look and a smile that tells her you believe she can do it. Say the word and wait again. When she takes her turn and says the word, share your excitement with her and respond immediately. If she doesn't do or say what you hoped for, try again another time. Remember that communicating together should always be an enjoyable experience for both of you.

Ideas for Choosing Goals

The following list may help you when you're choosing communication goals for your child. When selecting words to help her communicate, always choose words that will make it easier for her to talk about what's important and meaningful to *her*.

Early single words

Important People: baby, names of family and friends, child's own name, Daddy, Grandma, Grandpa, Mommy, names of pets

Food, Drink and Mealtime: apple, banana, bread, candy (or sweet), cheese, chips (crisps), cookie (biscuit), cracker, french fries (chips), hamburger, hot dog, juice, milk, pizza, water

Body Parts: belly button, ear, eye, hand, mouth, nose, finger, foot, toe, tummy

Clothing: bib, boots, coat, diaper, hat, pajamas, shoe, sock

Household Objects: bed, blanket, bottle, computer, cup, door, garbage (or rubbish), keys, light, TV

Outside Objects and Places to Go: flower, park, rain, school, sky, snow, store, swing

Animals: bear, bee, bird, bug, bunny, butterfly, cat, dog, kitty, lion, monkey

Vehicles: bike, boat, bus, car, fire truck (or fire engine), plane, train, truck (lorry)

Toys and Play Routines: ball, blocks, book, bubbles, dolly, patty cake (or pat-a-cake), peekaboo

Action Words: bang, blow, catch, clap, dance, drink, eat, fall, fly, go, jump, kick, kiss, open, peek, pour, read, run, sing, sit, sleep, stop, swing, throw, tickle, wash

Words That Describe: all done, all gone, big, broken, clean, cold, dirty, dry, hot, little, more, nice, off, on, pretty, sleepy, smelly, sore, stinky, wet, yucky

Words That Describe Time: morning, night, now, today, tomorrow, tonight

Words That Express Feelings: angry, happy, mad, sad, scared, sick, tired

Location Words: behind, down, here, in, on, out, over, there, under, up

Social Words: bye-bye, hi, I love you, night-night, no, okay, sorry, uh-oh, yes

Words That Express Belonging: my, mine, Mommy's, horse's

Question Words: what? where? who?

Two-word sentences

"More" + action or object: More swing, More jump, More story, More juice

"Want" or "Need" + person, object or action: Want juice, Need teddy, Want up

"No" + object, person or action: No bed, No juice, No eat

Describing disappearance: Cookie all gone, No more chips

Word that describes + object/person: Big ball, Dirty pants (or trousers), Banana all gone, Hot tea

Word that expresses belonging + object or person: My Daddy, Mommy chair

Object or person + action: Baby sleep, Mommy kiss, Computer on, Doggie woof

Action + object or person: Throw ball, Open door, Blow bubble, Kiss baby

Object or person + location word: On head, In bed, Under table, Horsie in

Action + location word: Open here, Go out, Slide down

Question word + object or person: Where bird? Who's that?

Three-word sentences

Person + action + object: Mommy kiss bear, Daddy throw ball, Jamie eat cookie

Adding location words: Horsie *in* barn, Put sock *on*, Hide *under* table

Adding words that describe: Want *big* truck, Car go *fast*, Make *big* mess

Early grammar

Add -*ing* to action words: Baby sleeping, Horsie eating apple

Add plural -*s*: books, shoes

Add *'s* to show belonging: Mommy's purse (or bag), Grandpa's car

Add *a* and *the*: a boy, the book

Add *is*: That bird is big. This tea is hot.

Chapter 7

Let's Play!

The most important part of playing with your child is having fun together. When you're having fun together, you're helping him develop his communication skills. In this chapter, you'll learn how to plan play activities that build your child's understanding of language as well as his ability to express himself. You'll also learn how to plan play so that, while the two of you are having fun, you're helping him reach his communication goals.

The Power of Play

Play is one of the most important ways that your child learns about the world. From playing with adults and children, your child learns how to interact and get along with others. Play also helps develop your child's problem-solving skills. By experimenting with toys, he'll make interesting discoveries – for example, which toys float in the bathtub and which don't. Playing with materials like paper, glue, playdough, finger paint and sand develops your child's creativity and imagination. But the best thing about play is that it helps your child learn many, many words and important ideas about the world. For instance, he learns that he goes *up* the stairs and *down* the slide. He discovers that a block is *too big* to fit into a little cup, and he pretends that the soup he's just made for you is *too hot*. Once your child understands these words and ideas, he may be ready to try saying them. It's easy to see that play skills and communication skills develop hand in hand.

The power of play comes from the connection it creates between you and your child. If you catch him at the bottom of the slide, laugh with him as he knocks over a tower of blocks or pretend to be the patient while he's the doctor, he'll want to keep playing with you for hours. Learning while he's playing with you is fun for your child and makes him want to keep the interaction going. That is the real power of play.

The power of play comes from the connection it creates between you and your child.

Get Organized for Play

If you can, plan ahead to make sure your playtime goes smoothly. Have all the materials you need next to you before you start. Use old shirts to cover clean clothes if the activity involves things like paint, sand, water or cooking. Cover tables with newspaper or a large garbage bag. Have a wet cloth or sponge nearby to mop up spills and make cleanup easier. Better still, have two sponges so cleaning up becomes a fun activity that you and your child can share. Then you can talk about the big mess you've made. Give your child a choice of just a few toys at a time, and then wait to see what captures his interest.

Alicia's mom has everything organized so she doesn't have to worry about Alicia making a mess. Now she can concentrate on having fun with her.

Get Involved in the Play

A successful play activity begins with you and your child interacting and having fun. To get things going, keep in mind these three strategies from previous chapters:

- Join in the play
- Create opportunities for your child to take turns
- Use play routines to SPARK an interaction

Join in the play

Find a way to join in with what your child is doing (to review this idea, see pages 35–38). If your child doesn't play with toys the way you expect him to, just "go with the flow." If he wants to put blocks *under* the truck

instead of *in* the truck or if he bangs the playdough and stretches it rather than making shapes, it doesn't matter. Let him explore and enjoy toys in his own way and see where the play takes you. The communication between you doesn't have to be about anything in particular. What's important is simply that you and he are communicating.

Mom gets her own toys and joins in making sandcastles with Brandon. They're having lots of fun and a long conversation about broken sandcastles.

Create opportunities for your child to take turns

If your child doesn't include you in his play even when you join in, you'll have to find another way in. The parents shown below all get involved in the play by creating opportunities for their children to take turns in the interaction. They do this by making sure their children *need* to communicate with them to get what they want.

Dad does the swing routine a bit at a time, and Robert gets a chance to ask Dad to push him again ... and again.

Grace's mom chooses a toy that Grace can't operate on her own. To keep the fun going, Grace has to ask her mom to blow bubbles.

When Dad holds on to the pieces Cameron needs to operate the toy, Cameron takes a turn by asking for the pieces one at a time.

Use play routines to SPARK an interaction

In Chapter 5 you learned that routines, especially people games, are ideal activities to encourage your child to take turns and learn language. Now you can create a new routine using a toy that interests your child. First, OWL to see what your child enjoys most about a particular toy or game. Then create a routine using the SPARK strategy that you learned in Chapter 5.

There's the cow. ... Moo-oo-oo!

When Robert finds the toy cow in her pocket, Mom makes the animal noise, which Robert loves.

Where'd the cow go?

Mom knows that Robert enjoys finding things she's hidden in her pocket, so she turns this into a routine. She hides a toy cow in her pocket and waits.

Where's the duck?

Later on, when Robert knows the routine well, he takes on Mom's role. He hides toy animals and then gets Mom's attention so she will look for them. Then, when she finds the animal, she makes the animal sound. The next step is for Mom to give Robert a cue so he starts to make the animal sound himself.

Explore and Connect with Discoverers

For a Discoverer, play is all about exploring. When a Discoverer explores something new, he puts it in his mouth. Then, when he discovers his hands, he learns that he can make things happen by touching, squeezing or shaking things. Give your child toys that he can hold on to, put in his mouth, touch, shake, bang, squeeze and pull. He will also enjoy watching things that look and sound interesting. Try activity centres with mirrors, doors and buttons; stuffed animals and other soft toys; rattles, squeaky toys and other toys that make noises; and big, soft blocks.

When a Discoverer plays with toys, he will pay attention only to the toy. He won't be able to focus on you at the same time. When you want to show your child a toy, get face to face. If you need to get his attention, shake the toy, rattle it, move it up and down or playfully touch him with it. Hold the toy close to your face, so he can start to learn to look at you and the toy. Respond immediately when he reacts to toys. This will help him make the communication connection. Imitate his actions and sounds. For example, if he bangs a toy on the tray of his high chair, you bang a toy too. Then wait with an expectant look on your face to see if he'll take another turn.

Jordan gets excited when he sees the "spider" crawling toward him.

Set Communication Goals for Play with Communicators, First Words Users and Combiners

Remember that before a child will say a word or a phrase, he must first understand what it means. The more language a child understands, the more thoughts and ideas he can share with you. That's why some of your child's communication goals should be to increase his *understanding* of language. You should also continue to set goals to expand your child's *expression*. This may mean helping him express more of the kinds of things he can already express at his stage of communication development, or it could mean helping him take a step toward the next stage.

Because goals for understanding and for expression are equally important, it's very often a good idea to work on both kinds of goals at the same time. **Within a single activity, you can help your child understand new words and ideas and help him learn to use a new gesture, word or sentence.**

How to choose communication goals

If you OWL carefully while your child plays, you'll have plenty of good ideas about which communication goals to choose. What does he love to do? What makes him laugh? What kinds of toys are his favourites? Once you've made a mental list of the things he enjoys most, fit your communication goals into those activities. For example, does your child like to pretend to put his toy animals to sleep? Then a good goal would be for him to understand action words like *lie down*, *wake up* and *snore* (he'll love to hear you pretend to snore). Eventually, he may learn to imitate these words. Remember: whatever your child loves to do will be what he wants to communicate about.

Help your child achieve his communication goals

To help your child understand or express a new word or idea, repeat the words again and again during your turn. Use gestures or visual helpers if you can. For example, open your arms wide for *big* or make a kicking motion for *kick*. Always match your words to the moment – talk about it as it's happening. It's also important to use new words in more than one situation. So if you introduce your child to the word *in* when you and he are having fun throwing a beanbag into a box, make sure you use the word *in* at other times too. Use it when he's *in* the bathtub, throwing something *in* the garbage or putting raisins *in* his mouth.

If you're helping your child learn to say a new word that he already understands, try to repeat the word at least five times during an interaction (see Chapter 6, page 87). That means repeating the word once or twice during your turn and then saying it again in your next turn (after your child has responded) and the one after that.

Setting Communication Goals in Three Kinds of Play

The rest of this chapter will be about setting communication goals within three different types of play:

- **Functional play** involves exploring toys and objects by banging, shaking, pulling and similar actions. It also includes physical play such as throwing, running and jumping.
- **Constructive play** involves constructing something with a plan in mind, such as building a tower from blocks.
- **Pretend play** involves make-believe.

Your child may enjoy one, two or all three kinds of play. Turn to the checklist "My Child's Stage of Play Development" on pages 129 and 130 to see what kind of play skills your child has. To learn how to set goals within each kind of play, read on.

Functional play

Constructive play

Pretend play

Setting communication goals for functional play

Functional play involves different kinds of repetitive movements. This includes banging or shaking toys, as well as filling containers and then emptying them. Cause-and-effect actions are a very important part of functional play. For instance, when your child switches a light or a music box on and off to see the effect his action has, he is using functional play.

Children at the functional stage of play try out various actions on sand, water and playdough. They enjoy the sensations of messing with mud, splashing in water and poking and pulling playdough and like to see what effect their actions have on these materials. During the functional play stage, children also start to use objects for their intended purposes. For example, they push toy cars back and forth. Running, jumping, climbing and ball games also fall into the functional category. Like all functional play, these outdoor activities help children improve their physical skills.

A note about using the goal charts in this chapter

As you read the goal charts in this chapter, keep in mind that the goals listed there are just suggestions. To get started, choose an activity and select *one or two* goals at the most from the column for your child's stage of communication. You may want to begin with one goal for understanding and one for expression. (All goals may be adjusted for use with signs and pictures.)

Make sure you do this activity often to make it easier for your child to learn the new word or idea. Also, try to choose some goals that you can carry over into other activities. For example, the word *go* can be a goal for when you're pushing your child on the swing, when the two of you are playing with cars and when you're chasing each other outside. If the goals listed don't include words that describe things your child enjoys doing, choose words that do.

Functional Play 1: Outdoor play

"Outdoor play" means running, jumping, hiding, chasing and other kinds of active play. When you and your child are playing outdoors, follow his lead. If he loves to run, hop and jump, join in. You can add some fun to a game of chase by giving him a choice of how he wants you to chase him. Ask him, "Do you want Daddy to *run* or do you want Daddy to *jump?*" Run and jump up and down on the spot so he knows what you mean. Let him choose with a gesture, a sound or words, depending on his stage of communication. As soon as he chooses in some way, do as he says! (If he wants to chase *you*, give him the words for *his* actions.) You may want to change the game to add more fun — for instance, jumping *high* or running *fast* or *slow*.

Goals for Outdoor Play with Communicators	Goals for Outdoor Play with First Words Users	Goals for Outdoor Play with Combiners
UNDERSTANDING:	UNDERSTANDING:	UNDERSTANDING:
• run, jump, hop	• run, run *fast*, run *slow*, jump *high*, jump *low*, hop	• *Daddy run, Daddy jump, Daddy hop, (Child's name) run, (Child's name) hop, (Child's name) jump, Jump over* (a stick)
EXPRESSION:	EXPRESSION:	EXPRESSION:
• Act out running, jumping or hopping to tell you what to do. • Imitate one of the words in the Understanding list above, when he knows what the word means.	• *run, jump, hop, up, down* (a hill), *on, off* (a low step)	• *Daddy run, Daddy jump, Jump over* (a stick), *Daddy hop, (Child's name) run, jump* or *hop*

Adam is a Communicator. His communication goal is to understand the word jump, and after hearing the word so many times in one activity, he now understands it.

Elizabeth is a First Words User, and her communication goal is to say the word high. She and Dad have been jumping low and high, and now she can tell Dad how she wants him to jump.

The goal for Tarik, who is a Combiner, is to understand simple sentences like, "Tarik is jumping," and "Daddy is jumping."

Dad is sure that Tarik understands "Daddy is jumping," so his goal now is for Tarik to try to imitate what he is saying, using a two-word sentence. So, Dad says "Daddy is jumping" and waits for Tarik to imitate him. It works.

Functional Play 2: Water play

Water play can take place in the bathtub or in a wading pool outdoors with a variety of toys. Toys can include containers of different shapes and sizes; containers with holes that let the water spray out; balls and toy people, animals and boats that float; and objects that don't float.

Observe your child. Does he like to pour water from cup to cup? If so, imitate him and say *pour* each time either of you pours. If he understands *pour* and he hears the word often enough, he may try to say it. If he likes adding liquid soap to the water so he can make bubbles, let him add the *soap* and *stir* up the water to make bubbles. Repeat the words again and again. If he scoops up the bubbles and claps his hands together, for example, imitate what he does and give him a word or two. Say "Clap bubbles! Clap, clap!" Let your child's actions help you choose your communication goals.

Goals for Water Play with Communicators	Goals for Water Play with First Words Users	Goals for Water Play with Combiners
UNDERSTANDING:	UNDERSTANDING:	UNDERSTANDING:
• *pour, water, wet, soap, boat, wash, bubbles, gone, in, out, splash*	• *under* (water), *fall in, fall off, fill up, full, wet, dry, splash, bubbles, cup, stir*	• *float, doesn't float,* • *sink* (when an object doesn't float), *heavy, full, empty, wet, dry*
EXPRESSION:	EXPRESSION:	EXPRESSION:
• Imitate one of the following words, when he knows what it means: *uh-oh, all gone.* • Use gesture or sound to request *more* of something (bubbles, toys etc.).	• *in, on, pour, boat, water, splash, bubbles, cup, stir, wet, dry, fall, full*	• *fall in, fall off, in water, on top of the water, fill* (name of container), *heavy, sink*

Functional Play 3: Games with balls

Most children love to play with balls. You can roll or toss large, soft balls gently to your child. You can also take turns throwing balls into a container. Use a large box or basket and take turns throwing balls, beanbags or blocks into it.

Goals for Ball Play with Communicators	Goals for Ball Play with First Words Users	Goals for Ball Play with Combiners
UNDERSTANDING:	UNDERSTANDING:	UNDERSTANDING:
• *ball, throw, catch, miss*	• *throw, kick, roll, bounce, catch, big, little, in, out, missed,* names for different containers (*basket, box,* etc.), *Move closer*	• *kick, roll, bounce, catch, big, little, I missed, high, low, fast, slow, far, near, harder, softer*
EXPRESSION:	EXPRESSION:	EXPRESSION:
• *Yay!* plus clapping (when he gets the ball into the basket) • Gestures for throw, kick, etc.	• *throw, kick, ready, catch, Go!, my turn, your turn, in*	• *Ball in, Bag* (for beanbag) *in, Ball missed, Here it comes, Move closer, roll, too far, too hard* (for when he misses)

Communicator: *Dad's goal for Megan is to understand the word* throw ...

... and to understand that Yay! *is a word for celebrating success. Dad will say* Yay! *in many other situations, too, to help Megan understand that it's not just a word to use in the beanbag game.*

First Words User: *Sofía's goal is to understand the word* throw *and ...*

... to understand the word missed. *Once she understands these words well, Dad will change the goal to encourage Sofía to try imitating them.*

Combiner: *Alicia and her mom have been playing this game for a while now and she can imitate "Bag in" because she's heard her mom say it so many times.*

Now that Alicia has imitated the words so often, she's ready to say them on her own.

Functional Play 4: Cars and trucks

During functional play, your child will "drive" his cars, trucks, trains and planes. Watch carefully to see what he likes to do with them. You can make this activity more interesting by creating paths, making ramps from trays or pieces of strong cardboard, or turning cardboard tubes into tunnels. You may need to show your child how he can drive a car up a ramp or through a tunnel and let it run down all by itself. You can also race two cars together.

Goals for Functional Play with Cars: Communicators	Goals for Functional Play with Cars: First Words Users	Goals for Functional Play with Cars: Combiners
UNDERSTANDING:	UNDERSTANDING:	UNDERSTANDING:
• *drive, up* (the ramp), *down* (the ramp), *stop* (when you put up the sign), *go, big, little,* vehicle names (*tractor, car, fire truck* etc.)	• *fast, slow, stop, go, <u>up</u> the hill* (when driving up the ramp), <u>*down*</u> *the hill, crash, in, out, broken, car, fire truck* • **Where** questions, such as "Where's the car?"	Note: Functional play often includes some pretend play at this stage. • **What will happen:** *The car's gonna crash.* • **Explain:** *The car can't go because it's broken* (or *because the car needs gas,* or *because it's got a flat tire*). • **Early questions:** *What happened?* (car crash), *Who's in car?* (man, Mommy etc.).
EXPRESSION:	EXPRESSION:	EXPRESSION:
• Imitate one of the words or sounds, knows what it me "brmm" (car nois *crash* (when cars one another), "wh cars go fast down *Uh-oh, Go!*	• Any of the words above that he has come to understand.	• Any of the words or sentences above that he has learned to understand. • *Car broken, Car fixed, Car need gas, Car going to* (place)

Setting communication goals for constructive play

When children get involved in constructive play, they do it to create something with a plan in mind. They build towers from blocks or constructions from Lego, or they make imaginative creations by gluing together materials like toilet paper rolls or pieces of cardboard. From exploring and experimenting during constructive play, children learn to solve problems and be creative. They learn from every step: planning the construction, working out how to fit pieces together and making sure the construction doesn't break or come apart. While they create things, they learn about size, length, shapes, patterns, weight – all ideas they'll use when they get to school.

Constructive play begins when children have developed the ability to understand and use words (or signs) and it continues for many years. It's important to let your child try to construct things by himself. If he needs help, show him how to do it just once or twice and then let him do it himself. He'll learn more by problem-solving on his own than by watching you do it for him.

Constructive Play 1: Building towers and other structures

Your child's first tower will be small and unsteady because he is still learning how to place one block on top of another. As his physical skills improve, he may begin to make more complex and interesting constructions. Your language will change as his constructive play becomes more complex. Watch to see what he does with blocks. Maybe he'll build a small tower and knock it down. Or maybe he'll make a low, wide building and put little toys inside it. Choose your goals to fit what he is doing.

Communicator:
Jamie's goal is to imitate "Uh-oh!" when the tower falls down. Jamie has heard his mom say "Uh-oh!" every time it has fallen. Now he can imitate it.

Uh-oh!

Uh-oh!

Uh-oh.

Down!

First Words User:
Brian's communication goal is to say down *when the tower falls down. Mom has said the word* down *every time it falls down, but this time she says "Uh oh" and waits. Then Brian says it all by himself.*

Goals for Building Towers (etc.) with Communicators	Goals for Building Towers (etc.) with First Words Users	Goals for Building Towers (etc.) with Combiners
UNDERSTANDING:	UNDERSTANDING:	UNDERSTANDING:
• *on, more, fall, block, down*	• *on top, tall, high, more blocks, my turn, big, little, tower,* names of things you can build with blocks *(train, fence, bridge)*	• *longer, shorter, bigger, taller* • Early questions, for instance comparing two towers: *Whose tower is bigger? Is it gonna fall?*
EXPRESSION:	EXPRESSION:	EXPRESSION:
• Imitate one of the following fun words, when he knows what it means: *wow, uh-oh, oh no, boom.*	• *on, fall, down, more, higher, my turn, again*	• *more blocks, really big (or tall), really long, mine, I made a (name of thing)*

Combiner: *Brandon's communication goal is to understand the idea of one thing being taller than another. So after hearing the word and seeing Mom point to the taller tower again and again, he can now point to the right one.*

Constructive Play 2: Playing with playdough

All children love playdough. It feels nice and soft and can be turned into so many different things. To encourage your child's creativity, avoid showing him how to make specific shapes and objects at first. Instead, give him tools like a roller, plastic knife, large stones, straws or even toy people. Children may move from constructive play to pretend play with playdough if they're at the pretend-play stage.

When your child is playing with playdough, it's very important to give him time to explore and experiment with it. Say nothing and just let him go to it. OWL to learn exactly what he's doing. Is he poking it, feeling it, rolling it, making a creation? Once you've learned what he's interested in, choose your communication goals.

Goals for Playdough Play with Communicators	Goals for Playdough Play with First Words Users	Goals for Playdough Play with Combiners
UNDERSTANDING:	UNDERSTANDING:	UNDERSTANDING:
• *squishy, roll, pat, cut*	• *rolling, patting, cutting, squishing, snake, balls, cookies, flat, poke, hole,* names of tools *(knife, roller), gone* (when rolling over something that had a shape)	• **Comparing things:** *long … longer, big … bigger, small … smaller, fat … fatter, thin … thinner* • *What did you make? What are you doing? Where's the (name of tool)?*
EXPRESSION:	EXPRESSION:	EXPRESSION:
	• *roll, pat, squish, flat, knife, roller,* names for what he's making *(ball, snake, worm, pizza, cookie* etc.)	• *I'm* + action *(cutting, squishing)* • *I made (ball, snake, worm)* • **Comparing things:** *Mine longer, Yours smaller*

Setting communication goals for pretend play

Children start pretending when they discover that one thing can stand for another. Just as a child learns that a word can stand for the real thing, he learns that a toy object can also stand for the real thing. For instance, the word *car* and his toy car both stand for a real car. You can see why pretend play and understanding of first words usually develop around the same time.

Pretend play is often about familiar, everyday activities that your child sees you do, such as sweeping the floor or talking on the phone. One of the best ways to encourage pretend play is to provide realistic-looking toys such as dolls, kitchen sets, blankets, bottles and toy cars.

At first, pretend play involves only one activity, such as pretending to eat or talk on the phone, which the child does only by himself. This usually starts at the First Words User stage, though sometimes Communicators pretend, too (especially if their understanding of language is more advanced than their expression). Pretend play really takes off in the Combiner stage, when a child may spend many hours playing house, store or doctor, imitating things he knows and has experienced. This kind of pretend play helps your child improve his communication skills because he needs to talk about what's happening or what's going to happen, why it's going to happen, how people feel and so on.

As your child gets more experienced in pretend play, he starts to pretend with objects that don't look exactly like the real thing. For example, he may use a stick as a pen or a ball as an orange. Later, he becomes able to use objects that look nothing like the real object. He just transforms them into what he wants them to be either by telling you ("This is my phone") or simply by using them in new ways (using a block as if it were a phone). Eventually, he no longer needs pretend objects to make believe. For example, he pretends to eat ice cream without holding anything in his hand.

Turn again to the checklist on page 130 to see how your child uses pretend play right now. When you choose goals for him, these will be the kinds of pretend play activities to use. As you'll see, the goal charts for pretend play give you extra ideas to make pretending even more fun.

Pretend Play 1: Cooking and kitchen play

Because they see us working so often in the kitchen, children enjoy pretending to cook and serve meals. If your child is just starting to pretend, his pretend play may be brief. Later, pretend play may involve a series of events, such as preparing food, then cooking or baking it, and then serving and eating it. If you are with him, he'll feed you, and if you join in, you'll see how much more he enjoys it!

Observe your child first to see what he plans to pretend about. Then join in, but let him lead the play. You can build his understanding of language and the world by adding some new ideas to the game. Once you add something new, though, OWL to see what he does before you continue.

Scott, a First Words User, is making soup for his Mom. Her goal for Scott is to help him say the words spoon *and* knife *and understand the action word* stir.

Mom adds to the play by talking for Bear, who has joined them for soup. Scott thinks this is great and goes along with the pretend game.

Communication Goals for Kitchen Play with First Words Users	Communication Goals for Kitchen Play with Combiners	Ideas You Can Add to Kitchen Play**
UNDERSTANDING:*	UNDERSTANDING:*	
• *hot, open, close* (oven, fridge and containers), *cut, stir* (tea, soup), *oven off* (switching off the oven when the food is ready), *pour, mix*, names of ingredients and utensils: *flour, salt, eggs, spoon, fork*	• Introduce a sequence of events – for instance, wash and cut vegetables, put them in the pot, pretend to add water, stir them, cover them up, stir again, serve soup to toys and to people, blow on it, talk about how delicious it is. (Make sure your child is doing this, not just watching you do it!) • Make tea – pretend to fill kettle, switch it on, put tea bag in cup, wait a few seconds, say "The water's boiling," switch off kettle, add water, ask "Can I have sugar?" or "Can I have milk?" More words: *stir, blow, too hot, drink*. Talk about the past – when your child has had tea before.	• Put a toy (for instance, a teddy bear) a short distance away from where the two of you are playing. Call the bear on the phone and invite him for dinner. Then "walk" him to the kitchen and tell your child, "Bear also wants soup." Include Bear in the dinner. • Talk to Bear. Say "Bear, do you like soup?" Pretend to be Bear and say (in a different voice) "I like soup. I want hot soup." Let Bear "talk" to your child. For example, in your Bear voice say "Jamie, you make good soup." Add "I need salt" and see if your child responds.
EXPRESSION:	EXPRESSION:	
• *mix, stir, hot, blow*, food names (*soup, eggs, pancakes, cookies*), tool names (*spoon, frying pan, pot, knife*)	• *hot tea, hot stove, hot soup, too hot, not hot, soup* (or *tea*) *all gone, no more tea, more sugar, no more soup, yummy cookie, yummy soup, drink tea, eat egg, cookies* (or *chicken*) *in* (oven) • *Do you want ____? It's hot* (or *cold, delicious, sweet, sour*, etc.), *Need more ____* • Names of foods: *vegetable soup, macaroni and cheese, Caesar salad, sushi*, etc.	• Pretend the phone is ringing. Say "Hello" and then "It's Grandpa. Grandpa says 'What's for dinner?'" Give your child the phone and see if he'll pretend to talk to Grandpa. If he doesn't or seems not to know what to do, *you* talk, showing him how to pretend to talk to someone on the phone about what's for dinner. • When you have finished your soup, suggest you and your child wash the dishes or put them in the dishwasher (use a box with thin strips cut out so little dishes fit).
* *These goals may be appropriate for Communicators with an advanced understanding of language.*		** *Your child may not understand all of these ideas, but if he seems interested, keep going. In time, he'll understand them and start to pretend that way too. Simplify these ideas for First Words Users.*

Mom's goal for Laura, a Combiner, is to help her learn to say two-word sentences using the word soup, like "Yummy soup" and "More soup."

Yummy soup. The soup's all gone.

Mmm. More soup for Mommy. Yummy soup.

More soup?

Uh-oh! I spilled the soup. It's a big mess. Let's clean up the mess.

Mom adds to the play by pretending to spill the soup. Laura is confused because she can't see any spilled soup. However, if Mom shows Laura how to clean up the imaginary mess with an imaginary cloth, Laura will eventually understand that you can make believe just by describing something.

Pretend Play 2: Cars, trucks, etc.

Create a road with bridges, stop signs, filling stations and tunnels, similar to the one described on page 120. This time, have a variety of vehicles that do different things (fire truck, ambulance, tractor, excavator, dump truck, school bus). Use little boxes to make buildings, stores and schools. Add some toy people so the two of you can create a story about them. Observe your child and see what he likes to do. Is he more interested in driving the cars or in doing something with the people? Follow his lead. Pretend with him and then add some new ideas just for fun.

Goals for Pretend Play with Cars and Trucks: First Words Users	Goals for Pretend Play with Cars and Trucks: Combiners	Ideas You Can Add to Pretend Play with Cars and Trucks
Driving to school		
UNDERSTANDING:	UNDERSTANDING:	
• *drive to school, stop car, open door, teacher, kids playing, See you later, sandwich* (for lunch)	• **Talk about the future** – *The little boy's going to school, He's going to play with his friends,* etc. • **Explain** – *(Name) doesn't go to school 'cause he's too little.* • **Feelings** – *(Name) likes school, He's happy at school.*	• Pretend to give the little boy a bag with lunch in it (you could give him a little bag made out of paper). • "Children" say hi to the little boy when he goes to school. Then they ask him to come and play.
EXPRESSION:	EXPRESSION:	
school, kids, drive, stop, teacher, lunch, bag	*Drive car, Drive to school, Stop car, Say bye-bye, Hi teacher, Drive home, Car go*	
Ambulance/hospital		
UNDERSTANDING:	UNDERSTANDING:	
• *ambulance, sick, sick man, lady, go to hospital, siren* (make noise)*, doctor, needle, make better, medicine*	• **Talk about the future** – *Ambulance driver's going to pick up sick man.* • **Explain** – *Man's going to hospital because he's sick.* • **Feelings** – *Man sad. He's got a sore leg.*	• Make a hospital out of a cardboard box. • Make little beds for patients out of cardboard. • Use doctor kit so your child can be the doctor and examine the patient. Show him how to use the stethoscope if he doesn't know how.
EXPRESSION:	EXPRESSION:	
	• *Man sick, Ambulance go hospital, Drive ambulance, Ambulance stop, Ambulance go, Man sick, Sore leg*	

Playing with your child gives you many, many opportunities for repeating the words you are helping him learn, as well as showing him how he can play in new and interesting ways. Playtime can be two minutes, 20 minutes or an hour. However long you have to spend with your child, there's so much to learn from playing together!

My Child's Stage of Play Development

Mark each statement below with *A* for always, *O* for often, *R* for rarely or *N* for never. When you're done, look for the activities where you've written an *A* or an *O*. These are activities that you can enjoy with your child now, so they're the ones you can build communication goals into. You can also try some of the other activities in each type of play, as long as they are just slightly above what your child can do now.

Functional play

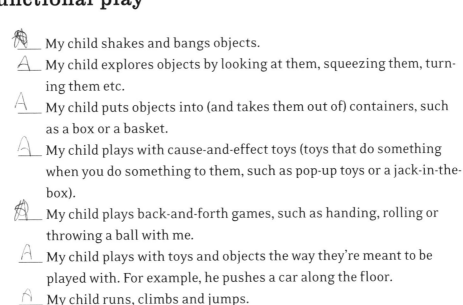

N___ My child shakes and bangs objects.

A___ My child explores objects by looking at them, squeezing them, turning them etc.

A___ My child puts objects into (and takes them out of) containers, such as a box or a basket.

A___ My child plays with cause-and-effect toys (toys that do something when you do something to them, such as pop-up toys or a jack-in-the-box).

A___ My child plays back-and-forth games, such as handing, rolling or throwing a ball with me.

A___ My child plays with toys and objects the way they're meant to be played with. For example, he pushes a car along the floor.

A___ My child runs, climbs and jumps.

Constructive play

A_ My child stacks blocks on top of one another.

R_ My child fits pieces into jigsaw puzzles.

R_ My child plays with clay or playdough, making specific creations from it.

O_ My child puts objects (such as Lego blocks) together to build things.

N_ My child makes creations using scissors, glue and materials such as fabric, cardboard, construction paper or dry pasta.

Pretend play

O_ My child pretends with toy objects that resemble the real objects. His pretend play is directed toward himself. For example, he pretends to drink from a toy cup or puts a toy phone up to his ear.

O_ My child does one pretend action at a time, and that action is directed toward another person or toy. For example, he might offer me the toy phone or pretend to feed his teddy bear a carrot.

O_ My child does the same pretend action with more than one other person or toy. For example, he pretends to give his doll a drink, then me and then his teddy.

O_ My child pretends to do activities that he sees me do around the house (such as sweep the floor, cook, mow the lawn).

R_ My child puts together two different pretend actions that he does to himself. For example, he pretends to pour a drink into a toy cup and then pretends to drink it.

O_ My child puts together two or more different pretend actions that he performs on others (people or toys). For example, he might feed his teddy, then give his teddy a kiss, then put his teddy to bed.

O_ My child uses a toy or object to pretend that it's something completely different. For example, he might pretend that a broom is a horse or a large cardboard box is a car.

N_ My child pretends without objects. For example, he might pretend to eat ice cream when there is nothing in his hand.

Chapter 8

Sharing Books

Books introduce children to new worlds. When you read to your child, you are helping her mind grow and develop. You are also enjoying the chance to snuggle up and share the fun of reading together. In this chapter you'll learn how to help your child learn language when you share books with her. You'll also learn some simple ways to lay a foundation for the reading and writing skills she'll begin to learn when she's older.

The Best Things About Books

Book reading is a special time for you and your child, when you both enjoy a feeling of closeness. But more than that, books connect your child to the world – her own world and new worlds. They transport her to interesting places and situations, many of which she has never seen.

The train goes Choo-choo, I think I can, I think I can, I know I can, I know I can.

Brian is fascinated by The Little Engine That Could.

One of the best things about books is that the pictures and words are always there to be read again and again. Unlike speech, which "disappears" as soon as we finish talking, the stories and words in books come back to us the same way each time we read the book. This makes learning new words and ideas much easier for your child.

The earlier you begin to read and tell stories to your child, the sooner reading will become an important and enjoyable part of her life. Reading aloud to your child is the most important thing you can do to build the knowledge she needs to learn to read. Try to make reading part of every day. Take a book along wherever you go – to a doctor's appointment, on the bus, in the car, to the grocery store ... anywhere. You can even take plastic or vinyl books into the bath.

When Brian goes on a train one day soon, his Mom will remind him about The Little Engine That Could *so he can connect a real train with the one in his book.*

Turn Book Reading into a Conversation

When you read with your child – regardless of her stage of communication – keep these guidelines in mind:

- Get face to face
- OWL and let your child "read" the book her way
- Give your child a chance to take turns
- Change the words in the book
- Use the Four S's – Say Less, Stress, Go Slow and Show
- Repeat, repeat, repeat

Get Face to Face: An important part of reading with your child is sitting close together and being able to see each other's faces. When you're sharing books, you may find it a little difficult at first being face to face and sharing a book at the same time, but it's important to find a way. This chapter's illustrations will show you a few ways to do this.

OWL and Let Your Child "Read" the Book Her Way: Story time is a time for conversation, not just sitting and listening. To get the most out of being read to, your child needs to be actively involved. When you think she's ready, let her choose the book, hold it and turn the pages. Once you've read what's on a page and shown her the pictures, give her time to look at the page and wait to see what she does or says. Spend more time on the pages she's most interested in. At first, your child will probably sit for only a few minutes when you're reading to her. If you let her "read" the book her way, she'll enjoy sharing books more and, over time, she'll be ready to sit for longer and look at books more often.

There's more than one way to read a book.

- You don't have to start at the beginning.
- You can skip pages or not finish the book.
- You can just talk about the pictures and not read the words.
- You can change the words.
- You can read the same book over and over again, even in one sitting.

Give Your Child a Chance to Take Turns: When you read to your child, you shouldn't be the only one communicating. Give her opportunities to take turns throughout the activity. Don't think of reading as something you do *to* your child. Think of it as something you and your child do *together*.

Birdie. The Birdie goes bye-bye.

Mom changes the words in the book and adds a gesture to make sure Graham understands.

Change the Words in the Book: Feel free to change the words in the book and to tell the story in your own simple words. Not all children's books are well-written, and some have words in them that are much too difficult for your child to understand. Change the words in the book so they're easier for your child to understand and so you can repeat them. The more often she hears the words, the more likely she is to understand them and try to imitate them.

Use the Four S's – Say Less, Stress, Go Slow and Show: It's better to **say less** when reading a book. Use familiar vocabulary and shorter sentences to help your child understand and learn. **Stress** important and interesting words and add sound effects that your child will enjoy, like the sounds of animals or cars. Make stories come alive by creating different voices for the characters and using actions and facial expressions to make them really interesting. **Go slow** – tell the story at a slower pace – to make it easier for your child to understand the words and to give her time to take her turn. **Show** your child what the words mean by pointing to the pictures as you talk about them and by using actions and gestures. Use toys or other objects to bring stories to life. For example, if you're reading a story that has a ball in it, have your child's own ball close by so the two of you can roll it and throw it – just like the characters do in the book.

Repeat, Repeat, Repeat: Children love hearing the same stories again and again – even after you've grown tired of them. Every time you read a story to your child, you have a chance to repeat the same words and sentences. But it's not enough for your child to hear the words many times. Particularly if she is a First Words User or a Combiner, she needs a chance to talk about what you're reading and to imitate the words. The more chances your child has to talk to you about the ideas in the book and the more she hears you repeat some of these words, the more her vocabulary will grow.

Make Your Own Books

Sometimes the books that children love most are homemade books. A homemade book is extra special for your child because it can be all about her and because she can help make it. This creates wonderful opportunities for your child to communicate and take turns with you. As you write the words beside the pictures, tell her what you're writing. Better still, ask her what she wants you to write. Here are three kinds of homemade books you can make:

✦ **Picture Books of Things Your Child Likes:** Your child is sure to be interested in a book you've made together about her favourite people, animals, toys or play activities. It's best to use photographs, especially if your child is still learning to recognize pictures. If she can recognize pictures from magazines or catalogues, you can use those. Give the book a name and write it on the cover – for example, "Hanifa's Favourite Things."

✦ **Interactive Books:** Make lift-the-flap books using construction paper. Hide an interesting picture under each flap. Or create a touch-and-feel book with different textures for your child to explore, such as pieces of wool, sandpaper or cotton balls.

✦ **Picture Books About a Special Event:** Take about eight to ten photographs of a family event – such as a trip to the zoo, getting a new puppy or a holiday celebration – and put them into a small photo album. If your child is able to recognize these pictures, she'll love looking at them and hearing the story, especially if it's all about her. If she's a First Words User or Combiner, she can even start to tell you the story.

Hanifa loves to look at this homemade book of her birthday party and talk with her mom about that exciting day.

Sharing Books Across the Stages

The way you read books to your child depends on how much language your child understands. Go back to the checklist at the end of Chapter 1, "My Child's Stage of Communication Development," and look at your child's level of *understanding* (not expression). For example, if your child's understanding is at the First Words User stage, but her expression is at the Communicator stage, choose books that are appropriate for First Words Users. Continue to build her understanding of language using books for First Words Users. Her goals for expression will continue to be at the Communicator stage.

Share books with Discoverers

It's never too early to introduce your child to books. Even if she just chews on the book – which she probably will – your child can still enjoy interactions with you and books. Because Discoverers won't understand the words or pictures in books, choose board books or plastic books that make interesting toys:

- **books with bright, colourful photographs or pictures** of people, familiar objects and common actions
- **books with rhyme, rhythm, repetition or simple sentences**
- **interactive books** – books that make sounds when you push a button or have different textures to feel or flaps to lift

That's the bunny's tail. Nice, soft tail.

Get face to face and show your child the book. Show her the parts that you think will interest her. Push the button beside the car and say "beep-beep!" or show her the brightly coloured dog and say "Look, doggie. Woof-woof!" Then observe and wait. See what she does. Follow her lead. If she makes a sound, imitate her. If she grabs the book and chews it or pulls it,

The part of the book Victoria likes best is pulling the bunny's tail, so Mom talks about the tail while Victoria pulls on it.

talk about what she's doing: "Num, num, you like chewing the book!" If she looks at a picture or at part of a touch-and-feel book, point to it and tell her what it is. Then wait again until she does something else or makes another sound, which you treat as her turn. Then take your turn. Show her something else in the book and keep the turns going.

Share books with Communicators

Now that your child understands some words and can recognize some pictures, reading to her is lots of fun for you both. She probably has some favourite books, which she wants you to read to her again and again. These are the best kinds of books for Communicators:

- **board books with thick pages** that are easier for your child's hand to turn
- **short books with rhyme, rhythm and repetition** – for example, *Brown Bear, Brown Bear, What do You See?* by Bill Martin Jr. and *Goodnight Moon* by Margaret Wise Brown
- **books with brightly coloured, realistic pictures** of people (especially children), animals, everyday objects and activities such as bath time, bedtime and eating – such as *Mommy and Me* by Neil Ricklen, *How Many Kisses Do You Want Tonight?* by Varsha Bajaj and *Big Baby Book* by Helen Oxenbury
- **interactive books** with things to touch or do such as make sounds, lift flaps or make pictures move – for example, *That's Not My Puppy* (Usborne Touchy Feely Books), *The Snowman Touch-and-Feel Book* by Raymond Briggs, *Where's Spot?* (lifting flaps to find Spot the puppy) by Eric Hill and *Cluck, Cluck, Who's There?* (lifting flaps to see eggs turn into chicks) by James Mayhew
- **books with nursery rhymes,** other rhymes and finger plays (such as "Eensy Weensy Spider")
- **homemade books** with photographs of your child
- **wordless picture books** – such as *Good Dog, Carl* by Alexandra Day

Take turns and add language with Communicators

When you read books with a Communicator, read slowly. Keep in mind that she is still learning what words mean. Communicators are very interested in pictures, so point to the pictures as you talk about them. Repeat and stress the words that you want her to learn. Pause regularly. Give her a chance to tell you something about the pictures on the page you've just read. If you wait expectantly, she'll probably make a sound or point to what interests her. Follow her lead, interpret her sound or gesture and then add your own simple comments.

Once in a while you can ask her a question *if* you're sure she has a way of answering it (for example, by pointing or by nodding or shaking her head). Don't ask too many questions, though. Book reading is a time for taking turns and having fun. Too many questions can make it less fun for your child.

When Adam and Dad read a favourite book about a little dog who hides, Dad waits for Adam to let him know he's found the dog under the flap.

Adam knows the book so well now that he can tell Dad what the dog says.

For fun, Dad added the word pat *and the action that goes with it to the story a few weeks ago, repeating it again and again. Now Adam pats the dog when Dad says the word.*

Set book-reading goals for Communicators

The most important thing to remember about setting goals for a
Communicator during book reading is that **first you must discover
what she enjoys most about the book**. For example, *All Fall Down*
by Helen Oxenbury shows children doing simple things like running,
playing and eating. If your child likes this book and enjoys copying
the actions shown in it, then a good goal for her would be to
understand the action words in the book, such as *jump*,
fall down and *sleep*.

To help her understand the word *jump*, for
example, repeat it many times as you both look
at the page where the children are jumping.
Then get up and jump with your child, saying *jump* again and again. Make sure you
use the word in other situations, too – for
instance if the two of you see someone else
jumping or a horse jumping over a fence on
TV. Once your child understands these action
words, as you read the book again you'll be able
to ask "Can you jump?" or "Where's the baby
jumping?" and she'll be able to respond. If she
still needs help to understand the word, give it
to her. This should feel like a game, not a test.

Dad's goal for Robert is to understand the words fall
down *and to imitate the word* uh-oh. *When Robert
sees the baby falling down in his book …*

… he and Dad fall down too. Robert soon learns what
fall down *means.*

And after hearing uh-oh *many more times, Robert can
now imitate it.*

When you choose a goal for **expression**, the key to helping your child achieve it is repeating the gesture or word again and again. For example, your goal might be for her to say "Shhh" and put her finger to her lips when she sees a picture of a sleeping child. With a goal like this, you should first make sure she sees the picture and hears the word dozens of times. After she's seen you use the gesture with the word many, many times, you can start encouraging her to imitate you. If she doesn't, repeat the word and gesture and continue. When she has learned to imitate the sound, give her a chance to say "Shhh" all by herself.

The next time you turn to the page, wait and see what she does. Look at her expectantly and give her a cue if she needs one, such as putting your finger to your lips or shaping your lips to say "Shhh" but without saying it. If she still doesn't say the word, say it for her and keep reading. Whatever happens, remember to keep the interaction fun!

Share Books with First Words Users

A First Words User is learning a lot about books. She holds books right side up and turns the pages. She enjoys books with interesting language, rhythms and sounds. She can often imitate the words you use as you tell the story and she likes to name the pictures. She can follow little stories and enjoys listening to them again and again.

You have many more choices about what to read to a First Words User, and she can enjoy a wider variety of books. She may like some of the same books as Communicators, but she'll understand them better and be able to talk about them. It's important to read new and interesting books to your First Words User, even though there will be some words and ideas she won't understand right away. With repetition and visual helpers, she'll understand them in time. These are the best kinds of books for First Words Users:

- **sturdy books with colourful, simple pictures and photographs**
- **books with fun rhymes, rhythms and repetition** – such as *Brown Bear, Brown Bear, What Do You See?* by Bill Martin Jr., *Mr. Brown Can Moo! Can You?* by Dr. Seuss, *Hand, Hand, Fingers, Thumb* by Al Perkins, *I Know a Rhino* by Charles Fuge and Mother Goose collections
- **interaction books** – like the *Spot* books by Eric Hill, or *Peek-a-boo!* and *Each Peach Pear Plum*, both by Janet and Allan Ahlberg

- **theme books** – for example, *Happy Baby Animals* by Roger Priddy, *Dinosaur Roar!* by Paul and Henrietta Stickland and *Tickle, Tickle* (children doing various activities) by Helen Oxenbury
- **short, simple storybooks** – for example, *Good Dog, Carl* (wordless book) by Alexandra Day, *The Snowman* (wordless book) by Raymond Briggs, *The Little Engine That Could*, *The Blanket* by John Burningham and *Go to Bed!* by Virginia Miller
- **family photograph albums and homemade books with photos**

Take turns and add language with First Words Users

What a First Words User learns during reading doesn't come just from hearing you read. Taking turns back and forth as you read is just as important. To make sure your child has a chance to think and communicate, don't rush. After reading every page, stop and observe her. Let her look at it as long as she wants. Wait and observe what she says or does. When she communicates with a word, a gesture or a sound, follow her lead, staying on the topic as long as she's interested.

To build your child's understanding, use books as a bridge to the world. Show her that what's in the book is part of her world too. If she has a doctor's appointment and one of her books is about going to the doctor, here's your chance to connect the doctor in the book with a doctor in your child's real world.

When your child goes to school, she'll need to be familiar with what we call the **language of learning** – the more complex kinds of language that children need to learn about the world. The language of learning is used, for example, to compare and contrast two things, to describe feelings, to provide explanations and to pretend and imagine. Long before her first school day, your child will start to learn this type of language from hearing you use it, especially when you read to her. Below are some suggestions for helping your child begin to understand the language of learning. Try to include this kind of language when you read to your child, but use only a few examples at a time.

- **Talk about things that have already happened**: "Remember, Dr. Brown looked in Sofía's ear." (Pretend to hold instrument and look in her ear.)
- **Talk about what will happen (in the future)**: "Mommy's going to the doctor. The doctor's going to check my eyes." (Point to your eyes.)

- **Describe, compare and contrast things:** "Sofía's ear was sore, but your ear is better now."
- **Talk about feelings:** "Sofía didn't like the needle. Sofía got scared." (Make a scared face.)
- **Talk about reasons, explanations (use *because* and *that's why*):** "Sofía took medicine because you had a sore ear." (Show the medicine bottle and point to her ear.)
- **Talk about imagined things:** "Does the baby have a sore ear?" (Suggest she check doll's ear.)

Teaching your child the language of learning is very important, even if she doesn't understand everything you say. Understanding always takes time.

Dad repeats the word ear *many times as he talks about an event in the past – what happened to Sofía the last time she was at the doctor's office.*

Dad creates some fun by pretending to have a sore ear (talking about imaginary things) and giving Sofía a chance to get involved.

*Dad uses the **language of learning**, connecting the book and the real world for Sofía. She doesn't realize how much she's learning – she's having too much fun in this interaction.*

Reading stories like *The Little Engine That Could*, *The Gingerbread Man* and *The Three Little Pigs* to your child is an important part of learning language. Hearing stories teaches children how to tell stories about themselves and things they've experienced. Once your child has heard a story a few times, she'll be able to join in, filling in a word. For example, when you say "Run, run as fast as you can! You can't catch me, I'm the Gingerbread ..." she'll fill in "Man!" When reading storybooks, take the time to pause and encourage your child to talk about the story.

Set book-reading goals for First Words Users

Many of your goals for a First Words User should be to increase her understanding of words and ideas, since she'll only talk about things she understands. You may find that your child learns some of her first words from her favourite books. Once again, your communication goals for your child will depend on which books she enjoys and what she wants to talk about.

Let's say, for example, that you read *Where's Spot?* to your child and she enjoys lifting the flaps to see if Spot the dog is there. This gives you a perfect opportunity to set some communication goals. One goal to improve understanding might be for her to understand and answer *where* questions, such as "Where's Spot?" The answer you give her, which she can then imitate, might be "I don't know" – until you find him in the basket, in which case you would say "In the basket." Another goal might be for her to answer yes-or-no questions like "Is he under the bed?" ("No") and "Is he under the stairs?" ("No"). Once she understands and can answer these questions, she may try to ask you a question on her own, using one word – for example, "Bed?" for "Is he under the bed?"

Scott enjoys looking at a book with pictures of farm animals, so Mom's goals for Scott are to say the names of the animals and the sounds they make.

Now that Scott's mom has read this book to him so many times, he can fill in the words quite easily.

You can also help your child learn location words such as *in* and *under* when reading a book like *Where's Spot?* Use these location words in many, many other situations until she comes to understand them. Once she understands the words, she may try to say them, especially if you wait expectantly after you say the word.

Sharing Books with Combiners

A Combiner can understand many words and ideas. This makes it possible for her to understand and enjoy more complex stories and to talk about the characters and events in them. She may also enjoy books that help her learn about interesting things such as dinosaurs or pets. She can now take an even more active role in book reading and can sit and interact with you for quite a long time. She'll enjoy acting out the story, as Tarik and his mom do.

Tarik's favourite book is Are You My Mother? *by P.D. Eastman. So his Mom brings the book to life by acting out the story with Tarik, making sure they take turns.*

Mom helps Tarik learn how to ask questions from the book as they act out the story.

Think of books as bridges between your child's world and the world she is learning about. Here are a few tips to help you:

✦ **Introduce New Ideas Through Books:** For example, if you read to your child about dinosaurs and then she sees dinosaur skeletons at a museum, she'll have some ideas about dinosaurs already. This will help her understand what she sees and hears at the museum. Then, when you get home and talk about dinosaurs while reading the book again, she'll have much more to talk about. She'll be much more likely to learn from what you say because she'll be even more interested in the subject. Also, use books to introduce your child to things she may never actually see or do, such as going on a rocket ship or riding a camel. You'll be building her knowledge, which she'll need when she goes to school.

✦ **Use Books to Build on Your Child's Experiences:** Books can build on information your child has already started to learn. If your child goes to the zoo and is fascinated by the polar bears, get a book about polar bears and read it to her. Talk about the bears in the book and the bears you saw at the zoo. The book becomes the bridge between your child's experience and the many new things to know about bears.

✦ **Use Books to Help Your Child Cope with New or Difficult Experiences:** If your child is going to do something for the first time, such as go to the dentist, prepare her for it with a book on the subject. Read it again and again to help her understand and get ready for the event. When you are at the dentist's office, talk about the book. "Remember how the dentist in the book asked the little girl to open her mouth wide?" When the visit to the dentist is over, go back to the book and read it again. Encourage her to talk about her own experience and see if it was similar to the one in the book. The *Franklin* books by Paulette Bourgeois and Mercer Mayer's books cover many difficult experiences that children have to deal with, such as having a new baby in the family, being scared of the dark, going to school for the first time and not wanting to go to bed.

✦ **Use Books to Introduce Your Child to Imaginary Places and Creatures:** Fairy tales and books about monsters, ghosts and other imaginary creatures encourage your child to use her imagination. When you and she talk about them, she's having fun while she's learning to use language to talk about imaginary things. This is an important type of language for children to know when they go to school.

The best books for Combiners:

- **books with predictable patterns and repetitive words or phrases** – such as *Are You My Mother?* by P.D. Eastman, *The Gingerbread Man, Brown Bear, Brown Bear, What Do You See?* by Bill Martin Jr., *The Eye Book* by Dr. Seuss, *Go, Dog, Go!* by P.D. Eastman, *Each Peach Pear Plum* by Janet and Allan Ahlberg or *I Know a Rhino* by Charles Fuge

- **simple stories with a main character** – Stories should have a clear beginning and ending and familiar themes that your child can relate to. Some stories may also talk about new experiences, such as having a new brother or sister, or going to school. The characters in the story may have familiar feelings such as being naughty or scared, and may find ways to solve these problems. Stories children enjoy are *The Little Engine That Could*, *The Very Hungry Caterpillar* by Eric Carle, *Mortimer* by Robert Munsch (very entertaining story with wonderful repetition), *50 Below Zero* by Robert Munsch, *The Snowman* by Raymond Briggs, *Where the Wild Things Are* by Maurice Sendak (a well-written book with some complex language, which can be understood because of the beautiful illustrations).

- **interactive books** – such as *Where's Spot?* and *Each Peach Pear Plum*

- **theme books** – with themes such as zoo animals, going to the doctor, going to the supermarket or things I can do myself

Take turns and add language with Combiners

Now that your child is a Combiner, expect her to interact with you and to take turns throughout the book reading. The more she and you talk about the book, the more she will learn. Read the books she enjoys, changing the words as needed to make them easier to understand and to allow you to repeat them more often.

Use the **language of learning** (see page 141) when reading to a Combiner. Your child needs to hear you talk in ways that encourage her to think, to solve problems and to imagine. This means talking about things that go beyond what she can see, hear and touch. Use one or two examples of the language of learning at a time. Don't overwhelm your child with information. Keep it simple and help her understand what you say by repeating it in many situations. Understanding will grow over time.

For example, if talking to your child about the book *Just a Mess*, in which a little creature tries to find his baseball mitt in his very messy room ...

- **Talk about things that have already happened:** "Remember how your room was messy yesterday?" (It's okay to ask some questions as long as you are not testing your child.) "All your toys were on the floor."
- **Talk about what will happen (in the future):** "Mommy's going to clean the kitchen when you go to sleep."
- **Describe, compare and contrast things:** "This room (in the book) is very, very messy. Your room is just a little bit messy."
- **Talk about feelings:** "Mommy was mad when your room was so messy."
- **Talk about reasons, explanations:** "The messy room is bad because you can't find your toys, like the little creature in the book."
- **Talk about imagined things:** "Let's pretend a fairy came and cleaned up your room. The fairy says 'It's all clean!'" (Pretend to wave a wand.)

The language of learning is what children need to know and use when they get to school. Your child needs to hear this kind of language so she can learn to use it herself. She won't understand everything you say when you talk about things in this way. But if you repeat these ideas often, use gestures and pictures, and discuss them in more than one situation, she'll eventually grow to understand them. In time, she'll start to use language the same way on her own.

Setting book-reading goals for Combiners

Goals for Combiners should still be to increase their understanding of words and ideas, as well as to help them learn to expand their word combinations. Use repetitive phrases in books to help your child learn to say two-word or three-word sentences that she can use in everyday conversation. For example, phrases like "Where's Spot?" (from the *Spot* books), "Are you my mother?" (from P.D. Eastman's book of that name) and "Be quiet!" (from *Mortimer*

Alicia enjoys a book about a little girl whose dog likes to sleep on the furniture. But the girl's mother always tells the dog to get off.

by Robert Munsch) are examples of phrases repeated again and again in books that your child may enjoy learning to say. Once again, your communication goals for your child will depend on what she really wants to talk about. Use the guidelines in Chapter 6, pages 105 - 106 ("Ideas for Choosing Goals"), to choose the kinds of sentence combinations you want to help your child learn. If you need to, change the words in the book so that you can repeat the sentences you want your child to learn.

Mom's goal for Alicia is to say "Kobi off _____" and "Kobi on _____." So she changes the words to make sure Alicia hears these sentences many times.

After hearing Mom repeat the two sentences again and again, Alicia starts to say them herself.

Lay the Foundation for Reading and Writing

Experience with books and stories gives children the building blocks they need to become readers and writers. They learn how books work — that when you read a book, you turn the pages, that you read from left to right and that the printed words actually say something. During book reading, children often hear language we don't use in everyday conversation. For example, in the story *The Gingerbread Man* there is a sentence, "No sooner had they reached the other side, than the fox tossed the gingerbread man up in the air." This type of poetic, more complex language is called the **language of books**. By hearing this kind of language from an early age, children will find it easier to read books when they're older.

Show your child that written words "talk"

There's a lot you can do every day to help your child get ready for reading and writing. One of the most important things is to show your child that the words on the page actually "talk." When your child's understanding is at the First Words User stage, you can start to use the following suggestions. They'll be most helpful, though, when your child's understanding is at the Combiner stage.

✦ **Point to the Words in the Book As You Read Them**: Run your finger along the line as you read. You can also show your child a word that she might be interested in. For example, if she likes the *Spot* books, show her the word *Spot* and say "This word says *Spot*" and continue reading.

✦ **Show Your Child Interesting Words in the Environment**: Point to words on street signs and buildings, for example, and tell her what they say. Show her a stop sign and tell her that it says "Stop," and explain why it's there. Show her the name of her favourite restaurant or the name of the street you live on. For example, "See, that says Victoria Street. Our house is on Victoria Street." Show her an envelope with "Victoria Street" on it and tell her it says the same thing as the sign outside.

✦ **Show Your Child How Written Words "Talk" in Your House**: Let her see you as you write a list of things you need from the supermarket. Then take her to the supermarket and use the list to remember what you need. Let her help you make a birthday card. Ask her what she wants to say on the card and write it for her. Let her scribble on the card as if she is writing her name. Help her type her name on the computer and show her that that word says her name. Point to the instructions on her medicine bottle and say "It says shake the bottle and then give Jesse one spoon."

Mom tells Cameron what the note says to help him understand that the note will tell his dad where they are.

Play with words

Playing with words means letting your child hear how words can be broken down into parts and put back together again. This isn't something you need to *teach* your child at this stage. She'll learn a lot just by having fun with words.

✦ **Sing Songs and Say Rhymes with Fun Rhythms**: For example, "This old man, he played one. He played knick-knack on my thumb. With a knick-knack, paddywhack, give a dog a bone, this old man came rolling home." Children enjoy the fun sounds of these songs, and without your teaching them they will come to learn that words like *knick* and *knack* and *bone* and *home* have similar parts.

✦ **Make Up Rhymes for Fun**: Find a word that rhymes with your name or your child's name. Make a game of it. "Is my name Mommy or is it Tommy?" "Is your name Kelly or is it Belly?"

✦ **Point Out Sounds That Are the Same**: "*Shoes* and *shorts* start with the same sound. **Sh-sh-sh**oe and **sh-sh-sh**orts. You're wearing **sh-sh**oes and **sh-sh**orts."

Encourage scribbling and drawing

Combiners are ready to begin holding crayons and scribbling on paper – an important step toward writing. Give your child simple art materials like thick crayons, markers and large pieces of strong paper so she can scribble and draw whatever she wants. Don't try to show her how to draw or how to print the letters of the alphabet. The most important thing is for your child to get used to holding a crayon and using it to experiment. Put your child's drawings on the fridge or on the wall for everyone to see. She'll be encouraged to do – and learn – more.

Reading with your child is something that you'll both enjoy and that will help her learn a great deal about the world. Try to read often and to read the same books many times. This gives your child a chance to learn from all the repetition. For a child, reading the same book again and again makes it feel like an old friend. This familiarity gives her the confidence to try to express herself. And reading the book with you creates a strong connection between books and being close to you – a connection that can help your child enjoy books for the rest of her life.

Chapter 9

Moving Forward with Music

Children love music. They often want to hear their favourite songs and musical rhymes over and over again. For children having a hard time learning language, music is an especially powerful way to connect and communicate. In this chapter you'll learn how to make the most of music by adding it to your child's everyday life.

The Magic of Music

Music brings language to life. By making language learning fun, music can help your child communicate. It can also help him in many other ways, by soothing, calming and distracting him and by changing his mood. Music has a place throughout your child's day, from a happy song you sing to him every morning to the soothing lullaby he hears as the two of you snuggle up at bedtime.

Don't worry if you're not "musical" or can't carry a tune. Your child doesn't mind how well you sing. For him, music is about fun and connecting with you. There are no rules about how to sing or which songs to sing. Sing the songs that your parents sang to you as a child. Sing songs about your child's everyday experiences – like "Twinkle, Twinkle Little Star" when you're looking at the stars or "Wheels on the Bus" when you're riding on a bus.

Sing songs for rainy days, snowy days and sunny days.

You and your child can enjoy different types of music – not just children's songs, but classical and popular music of all kinds. When buying music tapes or CDs, look for music that is sung at a slower pace. This will give your child a chance to really hear the words and even participate in the song.

Your child may also enjoy toys that play music when you turn them on or wind them up. But he'll probably have the most fun making his own music with instruments that you buy or make from objects in your home. You can use pots or boxes as drums and spoons as drumsticks. Make shakers by putting rice or beans in closed food containers. Be sure to make one for yourself so you can make music (and noise) together!

Movement is a natural part of music – and children love to move. Try adding movement to your daily routines and activities. Sing a song while you march into the house together or hop into the kitchen to get a drink of juice.

As your child develops, the types of songs and rhymes he enjoys will change. The way he responds to music will change, too. Go to the "Getting in Tune" checklist on pages 164 and 165 to learn how your child can participate in musical activities at his stage. When you've completed the checklist, take a look at the section that follows it for suggestions of songs and rhymes that he might enjoy. Then, keep reading this chapter to find out how to use music to help him communicate to the best of his ability.

A spoon and a pot make a perfect drum so you and your child can sing and make your own music together.

Taking Turns with Music

Music is one of the best ways to get an interaction going and keep it going. Once your child knows a song, he knows what's going to come next. That helps him figure out when and how to take his turns.

Your child's ability to take turns in musical activities develops over time:

- In the beginning, when you sing to your child, he'll watch you closely and move his body to show you he likes the song.
- Later on, he'll begin to recognize songs and rhymes. As you're starting a song, he'll get excited, smile, move his body, or become quiet and look at you.
- In time, he'll learn to take a turn by doing one or two of the song's actions or by saying some sounds and words. He may need you to show him how to do the actions before he tries them himself.
- As his communication develops, he'll be able to participate more and more in the activity by taking turns throughout the song with actions, sounds and words.
- Eventually, he may start an interaction by asking for a specific song or rhyme with a sound, an action, a word or a sign.

The first step to taking turns with music is to follow your child's lead. Get face to face and OWL to see how he's responding when you make music with him. Tune in to his moods. If he's upset or unwell, choose a soothing song. If he's full of energy, sing a song with lots of fun sounds and movement. Sing songs that go with whatever your child is doing or is interested in. Respond immediately to his messages, imitating his actions, facial expressions, sounds and words. Interpret his messages, including his requests for you to sing the song again or to sing another song.

SPARK an Interaction with a Music Routine

Once your child is familiar with a song or rhyme, create a music routine that will give him plenty of opportunities to take turns. Use the SPARK strategy you learned in Chapter 5.

Start the music routine the same way each time. If your child knows the rhyme "Humpty Dumpty," for example, sit on the floor with your knees up, hold your arms out and say "Let's do 'Humpty'!"

Plan your child's turn. At different points in the song, your child can take his turn

- to request a high point (for example, falling down at the end of "Ring Around the Rosie") or to fill in a word at the end of a line
- to request that you repeat the song or rhyme
- to start an interaction by asking for a specific song or rhyme

When planning what your child could do or say to take his turn, refer to the section "Choosing Communication Goals" on pages 99–106.

Adjust the routine to create an opportunity for your child to take a turn. Slow down the words and pause to cue your child that his turn has come. It's important to wait expectantly, as Robert's Mom does:

Robert's mom pauses before the high point of "Humpty Dumpty" ...

... which lets Robert know he should take his turn if he wants her to move on to the fun part.

It's okay to be a little silly when adjusting a music routine. Make a deliberate mistake and then wait for your child to tell you what's wrong.

If your child doesn't take his turn after you wait, give him a cue. Then wait again. If he still doesn't take his turn, take it for him and continue with the routine. (To review ways to cue your child, go back to "Cue Your Child to Take a Turn" in Chapter 4.)

Repeat the same actions, sounds and words. Repeat the song or rhyme again and again – over several days or weeks – until your child knows it well and can take his turn successfully.

Keep the routine going. At the end of the song or rhyme, pause and OWL to see if your child wants to do it again. If he lets you know that he wants to keep going, follow his lead and start the routine all over again. Keep the interaction going as long as your child is enjoying it and is actively involved. If your child has had enough, follow his lead and say "No more" or "All done."

Highlight Language in Songs and Rhymes

Songs and rhymes are a great way to add language for Communicators, First Words Users and Combiners. When your child learns "Head and Shoulders, Knees and Toes," he learns the names of parts of his body. "Old MacDonald" helps him learn animal names and sounds. Songs and rhymes contain action words, such as *hop* in "Sleeping Bunnies." They also have location words, such as *high* in "Twinkle, Twinkle Little Star" and *down* in "Ring Around the Rosie."

Use the Four S's

There are ways to sing to your child that help him take turns and learn new words. **It's not just what you sing, it's how you sing it.** Start by using the Four S's.

Say Less: Shorter songs with familiar words are best. If a song has a difficult word or a word you don't think your child will understand, then change it. For example, sing "Head and *tummy*, knees and toes" because *tummy* is an easier word for your child than *shoulders*. You can also shorten the names of songs to make them easier for your child to request, as Brian's mom has done.

Stress Important Words: Help your child learn important words in songs and rhymes by making them stand out. Sing the words a little slower and louder, or pause before an important word. For example, you could sing "Twinkle, twinkle little ... *star*."

Brian's mom shortened the name of the rhyme "Sleeping Bunnies" to "Bunny" with a hopping action. Now that's how Brian asks for the song.

Go **S**low: Make it easier for your child to learn a song by singing slowly. Songs and rhymes are often sung or spoken so quickly that children don't have a chance to really hear the words. A slower pace also gives your child the time he needs to take his turn.

Show: The actions that are part of songs and rhymes are natural visual helpers that help your child in three ways.

Visual helpers show your child what words mean: Actions work very well as visual helpers, such as when you fall *down* in "Ring Around the Rosie" and roll your hands *round and round* in "Wheels on the Bus." When paired with the words, these actions help your child learn what the words mean.

Old MacDonald had a farm Ee-eye, ee-eye, oh! And on this farm he had a ...

Pig.

Pictures and objects are another kind of visual helper. For example, you could play with a toy bus while you sing "Wheels on the Bus" or with toy farm animals while you sing "Old MacDonald." Puppets also work well as visual helpers and children often love to use them. The puppet can sing along with you and help your child learn some of the words and actions in the song.

Scott's dad uses puppets to help Scott learn the names of animals and the sounds that they make.

Visual helpers help your child start interactions: Once your child is familiar with a visual helper and the song it goes with, leave the visual helper out where he can see it. He may start an interaction by picking up a toy or a picture to tell you what he wants to listen to or sing.

Visual helpers help your child understand choice questions: Until your child can ask for a song all by himself, give him a choice of two songs. For example, if your child is a Communicator, show him pictures of a spider and a bus, which you have used during "Eensy Weensy Spider" and "Wheels on the Bus." Then ask "Want to sing 'Eensy Weensy Spider' or 'Wheels on the Bus'?" – pointing to the pictures of the spider and the bus as you say the words. Then sing the one he chooses.

Give your child a choice of two songs using pictures he's seen before: "Want 'Spider' or 'Bus'?"

Make Up Songs Especially for Your Child

Some of the best songs are the ones you create especially for your child. An easy way to do this is to put your child's name into a familiar song. You can also make up songs about what your child is doing or what he enjoys. All you need to do is change some of the words of a song that you know. Once you've made up a song, you can use it in many different ways. You can turn it into a music routine to help him finish a task. You can sing it and take turns. You can stress certain words to help him learn new words. You can even use the song to make a situation less stressful.

Where is Parker?
Where is Parker?
Meow, meow, meow!
Meow, meow, meow!
Come out and play.
Come out and play.
Now, now, now!
Now, now, now!

Borrowing the tune of "Frère Jacques," Brian's mom makes up a song that matches what Brian is doing now – looking for his cat, Parker.

This is the way we buckle you up,
buckle you up, buckle you up.
This is the way we buckle you up.
Click, click, click!

Hanifa hates being buckled into her car seat, so her Dad makes up a song about it to the tune of "Here We Go Round the Mulberry Bush."

Recipe for a song

- Choose a simple, familiar tune or make up your own melody. Here are a few familiar ones: "If You're Happy and You Know It," "Row, Row, Row Your Boat," "Frère Jacques," "Mary Had a Little Lamb."
- Make up a song about things that are familiar or interesting to your child.
- Make sure there are no more than 10 different words in your song.
- Choose meaningful, useful words that your child understands.
- Put words that you've chosen as communication goals at the ends of lines in the song. This is where it's easiest for him to take a turn and say (or sign) the word.
- Add simple actions to the song.

Making Music at Different Stages

Music with Discoverers

The rhythm, melody and movement in songs and rhymes capture the attention of Discoverers. Music routines are one of the best ways to get an interaction going with children at this stage. Choose a time when your child is quiet, alert and ready to interact. As you sing to him, look right into his eyes and use lots of animation and facial expression so he knows you're singing to him. OWL and imitate his sounds and movements if he responds. Once he knows a song or a rhyme well enough to know what the next step is, stop just before the high point or at the end and *wait* for him to react in some way. Give him plenty of time. Keep eye contact and cue him with your facial expression and body language while you count silently to 10.

Interpret anything he does as his turn. It could be faster breathing, kicking feet, a smile, a wiggle or a sound. Respond immediately and continue the song to help him make the "communication connection" – so he learns that what he does can make things happen. Add language by making comments like "You want to do Pat-a-Cake again, don't you?" or "I think you've had enough of Peekaboo."

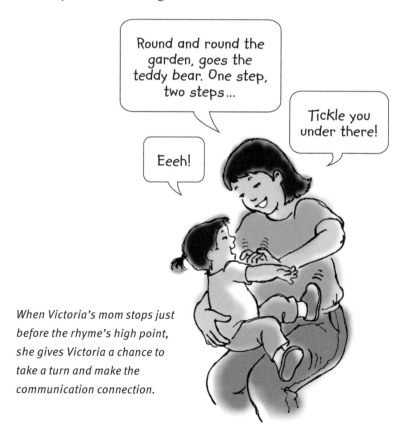

When Victoria's mom stops just before the rhyme's high point, she gives Victoria a chance to take a turn and make the communication connection.

Music with Communicators

A Communicator enjoys songs with actions, such as clapping in "Pat-a-Cake" or rocking back and forth in "Row, Row, Row Your Boat." Your child may hum or make sounds when you sing to him. He may bounce or sway to the music. He may participate by doing the actions along with you. Better still, he may fill in actions or sounds when you pause and wait for him to take a turn.

Here are some communication goals for Communicators:

- request the high point of a song or rhyme
- request that a song or rhyme continue or be sung again
- fill in a missing action or sound
- ask for a specific song using a sound or a visual helper

> Ring around the rosie, A pocketful of posies, Hush-a, Hush-a, We all fall...

> Duh.

Elizabeth's communication goal is to make a sound for down *in "Ring Around the Rosie." As soon as Elizabeth fills in the missing word, everyone will fall to the ground.*

The best way to help a Communicator participate in a song is to let him fill in an action or sound at the end of a line. When deciding on a communication goal of this kind, choose a sound or action that's interesting, useful and fun for him to learn. For example, if you leave out the word *there* in the sentence "Tickle you under *there*" (in the "Round and Round the Garden" rhyme), he may make a sound or even say "deh." This would be a wonderful first step toward learning the word. Keep in mind that when you pause to let your child fill in the action or sound, you may need to wait for several seconds. If he doesn't take a turn, take his turn for him and finish the song.

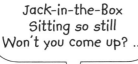

> Jack-in-the-Box Sitting so still Won't you come up? ...

> Yes, I will!

Jamie's communication goal is to fill in the jumping action at the end of the rhyme. He's become very good at this!

Music with First Words Users

A First Words User may be able to ask for songs by name, using a single word. He starts to connect songs with his daily experiences and routines. If your child is beginning to pretend in his play, you can pretend with him in songs and rhymes – for instance, pretend to drive a bus while singing "The Wheels on the Bus."

Communication goals for a First Words User can be for him to take turns to do one of the following things:

- ask for the music to continue or the song to be sung again
- fill in a missing word at the end of a line
- start an interaction to tell you what he wants to sing

To take these turns he should use a word (or a sign or a picture). When deciding on his communication goal, choose a word that's interesting, useful and fun for him to learn. Try to think of words he can use in other situations, such as *hands* in "If you're happy and you know it, clap your hands." Make sure your child is familiar with both the song and the word you're expecting him to say.

More! ... Grace wants more Spider. "The eensy weensy spider ...

Grace's communication goal is to use a sign for more. Dad waits to give her a chance to do it — and she does.

Twinkle, twinkle, little ...

... tar!

Scott's communication goal is to say the word star. *His mom points to real stars and then waits for him to fill in the word.*

Music with Combiners

A Combiner begins to carry a tune and might sing some of the repetitive parts of a song. He begins to use songs and rhymes in his pretend play. For example, he may make his stuffed animals dance to the music. You can help your child use songs to pretend, as Brandon's dad does.

Communication goals for Combiners can be to use two- or three-word sentences to do one of these things:

- ask for a music routine to continue
- fill in two or three words that come at the end of a line
- start an interaction by talking about a song or rhyme, or requesting it

Use songs or rhymes to help your child learn a variety of words. For example, if you want to help him learn more action words — such as *hop*, *eat* or *clap* — then build these into your goals. You may want to help your child learn words to describe things — like *big*, *small* or *funny*. If you can't find a song that uses these words, make up your own.

Maybe that's the Eensy Weensy Spider.

Yeah.

Brandon's dad encourages Brandon to use his imagination and think about the spider in a new way.

Wake up little bunny and ...

Hop, hop, hop!

Alicia's mom has built in an opportunity for Alicia to fill in the words at the end of the line. At the same time Alicia is learning a new action word.

Getting in Tune

This checklist will help you learn how to use songs and rhymes to help your child communicate and learn language. Each statement in the list describes one way in which a child can participate in musical activities. As you read the statements, next to each one put the letter that shows how well it describes your child.

A = Always
O = Often
R = Rarely
N = Never

Discoverers:

____ My child responds to music by becoming quiet.

____ My child responds to music by increasing his activity (for instance, kicking his feet) or making sounds.

____ My child watches my face when I sing to him.

____ My child makes sounds when I sing to him.

____ My child reacts in some way when I pause, look at him and wait after a song is over.

Communicators:

____ My child performs song actions along with me such as clapping or falling down (in "Ring Around the Rosie").

____ My child plays toy instruments – for instance, he bangs on a toy drum.

____ My child sings along with me by making simple sounds like "ba," "ma" or "da."

____ My child imitates sounds and sound patterns in songs and rhymes.

____ My child moves his body to the music.

____ My child uses a sound or an action to ask for a music routine to continue or to request the high point.

____ My child takes a turn in a song or a rhyme by filling in a missing action or sound.

First Words Users:

___ My child uses the word *more* or *again* to ask me to repeat a song.

___ My child names a song that he hears – with one word.

___ My child asks for a song or a rhyme using a specific word, such as "Bunny" for "Sleeping Bunnies."

___ My child fills in a missing word or sign that comes at the end of a line in the song or rhyme.

___ My child plays toy instruments along with music.

Combiners:

___ My child takes turns with two or more words in music activities. For example, he might say "More 'Bus.'"

___ My child fills in two or three missing words at the end of a line in a song. For example, if I sing "Tip me over and ...," my child will say "Pour me out.")

___ My child has begun to carry a tune.

___ My child sings songs to himself with one or two recognizable words.

___ My child associates songs and rhymes with everyday activities and experiences. For example, if we see a spider on the ground he may say "Eensy Weensy Spider."

Popular Children's Songs and Rhymes

The types of songs and rhymes that your child enjoys will change as he develops. The songs and rhymes below begin with those that children enjoy at earlier stages of their communication development.

"Humpty Dumpty"

Humpty Dumpty sat on a wall. *(Sit your child up on your knees.)*
Humpty Dumpty had a great *(Pause and wait here.)* ... fall!
(Bring your knees down quickly.)
All the king's horses and all the king's men
Couldn't put Humpty together again.

"Row, Row, Row Your Boat"

*(Sit across from your child and join both hands,
then rock back and forth as you sing the song.)*

Row, row, row your boat
Gently down the stream.
Merrily, merrily, merrily, merrily
Life is but a dream.

"Head and Shoulders"

Head and shoulders
Knees and toes, knees and toes, knees and toes.
Head and shoulders, knees and toes
Eyes, ears, mouth and nose.

Help your child learn the words for parts of the body by pointing to the body part as you sing the word.

"This Is the Way We Wash Our Face"
(Sing to the tune of "Here We Go Round the Mulberry Bush.")

This is the way we wash our face, wash our face, wash our face.
(Sing while you wash your child's face.)
This is the way we wash our face, early in the morning
(or "before we go to bed").

Other verses can include the following (or change the words to match your activity): ... brush our teeth, ... put on shoes, ... stir the juice, ... pick up toys.

"If You're Happy and You Know It"
If you're happy and you know it, clap your hands. *(clap, clap)*
If you're happy and you know it, clap your hands. *(clap, clap)*
If you're happy and you know it, and you really want to show it,
If you're happy and you know it, clap your hands. *(clap, clap)*

Other verses:
... stamp your feet *(stamp, stamp)*
... touch your nose *(touch your nose)*
... shout "hooray!" *(put your hands in the air)*

"Eensy, Weensy Spider"
The eensy weensy spider climbed up the water spout.
   (Put your fingers together to pretend spider is crawling up.)
Down came the rain and washed the spider out.
   *(Put hands up and then bring hands down quickly as
   you say down to pretend rain is falling.)*
Out came the sun and dried up all the rain.
   (Put arms in a circle above your head to show the sun.)
And the eensy weensy spider climbed up the spout again.
   (Put your fingers together to pretend spider is crawling up again.)

"Sleeping Bunnies"

(Child and parent lie on floor with eyes closed or child lies on floor with eyes closed and parent sits beside him.)

See the sleeping bunnies
Sleeping till it's noon.
Come and help us wake them
With this happy tune.
Oh, so still. Are they ill?
(Pause and wait here.)

Wake up, little bunnies and hop, hop, hop. *(Jump up and hop.)*
Wake up, little bunnies and hop, hop, hop.
Wake up, little bunnies and stop, stop, stop. *(Stop jumping.)*

"The Wheels on the Bus"

The wheels on the bus go round and round, *(Move your hands in a circle motion.)*
Round and round, round and round.
The wheels on the bus go round and round,
All through the town.

Verses:

- The people on the bus go up and down ... *(Bump your child up and down on your knees.)*
- The door on the bus goes open and shut ... *(Start with the palms of your hands together and then open hands when you say* open *and put hands together again when you say* shut.)
- The horn on the bus goes "Beep beep beep!" ... *(Pretend you're honking a horn.)*
- The babies on the bus go "Wah, wah, wah!" ... *(Pretend you're crying.)*
- The mommies on the bus go "Sh, sh, sh!" ... *(Put your finger up to your lips.)*
- The wipers on the bus go "Swish, swish, swish!" ... *(Make your hands go side to side like windshield wipers.)*

References

Agin, M., Geng, L., Nicholl, N. (2003). *The late talker: What to do if your child isn't talking yet.* New York: St. Martin's Press.

Allen, K., and Marotz, L. (1994). *Developmental profiles: Pre-birth through eight* (2nd ed.). Albany, N.Y.: Delmar Publishing Inc.

Armbruster, B., Lehr, F., Osborn, J. (2003). *A child becomes a reader.* Portsmouth, N.H.: National Institute for Literacy with RMC Research Corporation.

Bahan, B., and Dennis, J. (1990). *Signs for me: Basic sign vocabulary for children, parents and teachers.* San Diego, Calif.: Dawn Sign Press.

Brooks McLane, J., and Dowley McNamee, G. (1991). The beginnings of literacy. *Zero to Three Journal.* Retrieved March 9, 2004, from Zero to Three website.

Fox, M. (2001). *Reading Magic.* Orlando, Fla.: Harcourt, Inc.

Justice, L. M., and Kaderavek, J. (2002). Using shared storybook reading to promote emergent literacy. *Teaching Exceptional Children, 34*(4), 8-13.

Lahey, M., and Bloom, L. (1977) Planning a first lexicon: Which words to teach first. *Journal of Speech and Hearing Disorders, 72, 340–350.*

Lerner, C., Dombro, M. S., Levine K. (2000). *The magic of everyday moments.* Washington, D.C.: Zero to Three.

Manolson, A. (1992). *It takes two to talk: A parent's guide to helping children communicate.* Toronto: The Hanen Centre.

Manolson, A., Ward, B., Dodington, N. (1995). *You make the difference in helping your child learn.* Toronto: The Hanen Centre.

Neuman, S. B., and Dickinson, D. K. (Eds.) (2002). *The handbook of early literacy.* New York: The Guilford Press.

Neuman, S. B., Copple, C., and Bredekamp, S. (2000). *Learning to read and write.* Washington, D.C.: National Association for the Education of Young Children.

Paul, Rhea (1995). *Language disorders from infancy through adolescence: Assessment and intervention.* St. Louis, Mo.: Mosby-Year Book, Inc.

Pawl, J. (1991). A book is a child's companion. *Zero to Three Journal, 12*(1). Retrieved March 9, 2004, from Zero to Three website.

Pronin Fromberg, D., Bergen, D. (Eds.) (1998). *Play from birth to twelve and beyond.* New York: Garland Publishing Inc.

Ratner, N., & Bruner, J. (1978). Games, social exchange and the acquisition of language. *Journal of Child Language, 5, 391–401.*

Roper, N., and Dunst, C. (2003). Communication intervention in natural learning environments: Guidelines for practice. *Infants and Young Children, 16*(3), 215-226.

Rossetti, L. (2001). *Early intervention for special populations of infants and toddlers.* Presentation at Toronto.

Schwartz, S., and Heller Miller, J. (1996). *The new language of toys: Teaching communication skills to children with special needs.* Bethesda, Md.: Woodbine House.

Sénéchal, M. Read it again, Pam! On the importance of repeated reading for the development of language. 6-1 to 6-9. In Girolametto, L., and Weitzman, E. (Eds.) (2003), *Enhancing caregiver language facilitation in child care settings.* Toronto: The Hanen Centre.

Sussman, F. (1999). *More than words: Helping parents promote communication and social skills in children with autism spectrum disorder.* Toronto: The Hanen Centre.

Tough, J. (1985). *Talking and learning.* London: Ward Lock Educational.

Vygotsky, L. (1978). *Mind in society: The development of higher psychological processes.* Cambridge, Mass.: Harvard University Press.

Warr-Leeper, G. (2000). *Helping kids discover and develop language.* London, Ont.: University of Western Ontario Press.

Watson, M., and Zlotolow, S. (1999). *More than playing around* (CD-ROM). Eau Claire, Wisc.: Thinking Publications.

Wells, G. (1986). *The meaning makers: Children learning language and using language to learn.* Portsmouth, N.H.: Heinemann.

Wetherby, A., and Prizant, B. (1989). The expression of communicative intent: Assessment guidelines. *Seminars on Speech and Language, 10,* 77-91.

Wetherby, A., Warren, S., Reichle, J. (Eds.) (1998). *Transitions in pre-linguistic communication.* Baltimore, Md.: Paul H. Brookes Publishing Co.

Wetherby, A. (1999). Babies learn to talk at an amazing rate. First Words Project (unpublished handout).

Wetherby, A. (2001). *Early identification and intervention with children at-risk for communication disorders under 24 months of age.* First Words Project (unpublished handout).

Wetherby, A. (2001). *Early identification and intervention for children at risk for communication disorders (to 24 months).* Presentation at Toronto.

Weitzman, E., and Greenberg, J. (2002). *Learning language and loving it: A guide to promoting children's social, language, and literacy development in early childhood settings.* Toronto: The Hanen Centre.

The Hanen Centre

Mission Statement

The Hanen Centre provides the important people in a young child's life with the knowledge and training they need to help the child develop the best possible language, social and literacy skills.

We do this by:

- creating programs that teach parents and other caregivers how to promote children's language development during everyday activities

- training speech-language pathologists to run Hanen Programs and to use Hanen's child-centred approach in their day-to-day work with families and teachers

- training community professionals to lead programs for parents of children at risk

- sharing information with professionals who support parents' and teachers' efforts to give children the best start in life

- developing outstanding, user-friendly learning materials

- conducting leading edge research in our field